CAPERS IN THE CHURCHYARD

ANIMAL RIGHTS ADVOCACY IN THE AGE OF TERROR

LEE HALL

Foreword by Jeffrey Moussaieff Masson

COVER PHOTO: *Gladys Hammond spent her entire life in the village of Yoxall, in Staffordshire, England. When she died in 1997, aged 82, she was buried in a cemetery behind the centuries-old Anglican church where she had worshipped.*

OTHER BOOKS FROM NECTAR BAT PRESS:
_____

Priscilla Feral and Lee Hall,
Dining With Friends: The Art of North American Vegan Cuisine (2005).

PUBLISHED IN THE UNITED STATES OF AMERICA BY

Nectar Bat Press
777 Post Road, Suite 205
Darien, Connecticut 06820

Copyright © 2006 by Lee Hall
Friends of Animals
Internet: www.friendsofanimals.org
Phone: (203) 656-1522

Book Design: Mark Zuckerman

Published 2006

Printed in the United States of America on recycled paper

ISBN 0-9769159-1-X

To Priscilla. And the zebras.

Foreword

I have never met Lee Hall. But I read her 2005 review "Interwoven Threads," a commentary, published in the University of California at Los Angeles Women's Law Journal, about Catharine MacKinnon's views on feminism and animals, and I thought: Here is somebody who can really *think*.

Now I have read her first book, and my opinion is reinforced. It is not only that Lee Hall thinks, but also that she encourages thinking in others. There is no experience so exhilarating as to read somebody who has thought about something more deeply than you have, and yet provides all the evidence that allows you to advance your own thinking. There is no greater excitement in travel (and mind-travel is just one version) than to move forward. Lee Hall moves us forward. I love her for it.

My activism, such as it is, consists exclusively of writing. I act by writing. I don't, generally, join marches, or write petitions, or lobby Congress or do any of the other things activists do. But in my own way I attempt to push the arguments further. After writing three best-selling books about animals, *When Elephants Weep, Dogs Never Lie About Love*, and *The Nine Emotional Lives of Cats*, I suddenly realized that all the arguments I was making about the complex and profound emotional lives of animals in our homes or in the wild applied just as strongly to the animals forced to live on farms. I did not want to think about this in any depth, for fear that doing so would force me to change my ways – for example, to give up eggs and dairy products. Nobody, I have discovered, likes making fundamental changes to the way they live; that is, what they eat, what they wear, how they transport themselves, even where they live. But I *did* think about the lives led by farm animals, the ways they were forced to live and what this did to their natural emotions. It was a wrenching experience, and culminated in *The Pig Who Sang to the Moon* – not, alas, a children's book. Sometimes it is good to force yourself to do something you would rather not have to do. In the imagination, at least.

I had not given much thought to activism that went beyond the conventional definition, and had rarely asked myself what I thought about people who were willing to put their own freedom, perhaps even their own lives, on the line in the struggle to make the public aware of the conditions under which most animals associated with humans live. Partly I did not *want* to think about it, and partly it seemed somewhat remote from my own concerns.

Lee's book forced me to think about it. I found myself agreeing with everything she wrote. I could see no up side to threatening people into accepting certain facts. I have an old and very strong opinion about emotions: they cannot be forced. It always amazed me that we could be so stricken (though stricken we are) when somebody does not love us, or desire us. Or rather, of course we are struck in our heart; but it is the next move that puzzled me (though I am as guilty as anyone else in engaging in the exact same behavior): demanding, pleading, hoping, praying that the offending party will come to share *my* feelings. I love you, you *must* love me. But feelings don't work that way. They are not amenable to instruction, even to reason, and least of all, it seems to me, to threat. "Love me or else" is rarely a winning proposition.

So to tell somebody who does not care that animals suffer, "you *must* care" seemed to me hopeless. Our asking will not make the crucial difference. What does? Well, I have always believed in the power of persuasion: *convince* them that reason is on our side. *Show* them what they are reluctant to see. Point your finger in the right direction and hope they look there.

But if they don't, what can you do? Suppose they are not convinced; they do not see what we see, or, even if they do, they just don't care. What is the next step? Well, according to some activists, the ones whom Lee Hall engages in argument, there is nothing left but to threaten, intimidate, frighten, or even, going a step further, *hurt* the other side (or still worse: threaten or hurt those people they care about). They hurt animals, the argument goes; now let them see what that feels like when the shoe is on the other foot. As they cause suffering, let them suffer in their turn.

Well, yes, that is something I have often fantasized about. I confess that there are times when I too feel *schadenfreude*, pleasure in another person's sorrow. Yesterday I heard on the radio that a hunter walked up to a doe he had just shot and that the doe, with her dying breath, threw her legs in the air and caught the hunter's shin, badly lacerating it. He was hospitalized. I did not feel in the least sorry for the hunter. I told the story to my kids, and they both agreed, even the four-year-old, "serves him right." I could not disagree. But if an activist tells me that I should deliberately go out and target hunters and attempt to harm them in the same way they are harming the deer, I would be appalled. (As a 14 year-old, I started an anti-hunting club: we would arms ourselves with BB guns and go out to where hunters were shooting birds, and shoot over their heads to make them leave. I can see that it would have been a short step to taking aim at the hunters, but it is a step I never took.) What I want the hunter to see is the harm he has done to a fellow sentient creature. I want him to feel compassion. But would I succeed in teaching him compassion if I behaved toward him in a violent manner? I find it hard to believe I would. Yes, he might be so frightened of my threats that he would cease hunting. I can imagine that I could change his behavior. But not his feelings.

And surely what we all want is for a *transformation* in consciousness to take place, not just a tinkering with certain mechanisms. The Buddhists talk about something they call *ashrayaparavirti*, a major turn of the ground on which one is standing. In short, we want an epiphany against hunting. If the hunter is somehow convinced that what he is doing is cruel, he will teach what he has himself learned to others, to his family perhaps. If he merely desists out of fear, he will not carry any kind of message to others, but will feel resentment, which is sure to find expression in some different act of cruelty. We want the hunter to have an epiphany, for the ground under him to move.

As I read Lee Hall, I realized that what interests me most deeply is how we can create these fundamental shifts in perception, or at least create the conditions that allow them to take place. How do any of us, I began to wonder, escape the confines of our socialization? When I tell people that our children are being raised as vegetarians (my partner and I are vegans, but our two children, aged nine and four, are hard to persuade), even friends often accuse us of "brainwashing" them into our views rather than letting them reach their own. But surely the vast majority of people are brainwashed on a daily basis – as to what they eat, wear, drive, read, see or engage in just about any other activity mediated by society. Surely the families that encourage their children to eat meat are as guilty as we are of "brainwashing" if that is what it is. Who amongst us grew up in any kind of environment free of these mental contaminants?

When I think of how I found my professions (all three of them), I realize that it is almost always a case of following the majority. At 18 I was in no position to know what I wanted to do with the rest of my life. I will probably be no more ready on March 28th, my 65th birthday! I may not know what I want, but I get better and better at knowing what I do *not* want. This is the essential part of becoming an adult, no matter how long it takes us. That is, maturity consists in the ability to reject, or – to put it a different way – to think through the mainstream view. Sometimes the majority is right (I accept evolution and many other things that I do not have sufficient personal experience to have a deep opinion about), but often it is wrong. I am convinced, for example, that *much*, if not all, medical opinion is deeply biased. I believe the same about education, and information on how small infants should be treated. I believe that *all* traditional psychiatry is wrong. And equally strongly, I believe that the traditional American diet is also wrong. I have fought my way to these beliefs by reading, thinking and having certain experiences. None of these insights came easily, nor did I achieve them happily. My life, like the life of just about anyone else, would be infinitely easier if I simply accepted *things as they are*. The mainstream is mainstream, after all, because *most* people believe these things, and our world is constructed around these beliefs. To reject them is to set oneself up for rejection by the mainstream. This is something every activist must learn.

I believe that in some activists (all of whom have deviated from the mainstream through their own thinking) there is a certain desire for revenge. As I said, I too feel it. I would love it if my prime enemies were to suffer some disaster that would justify my beliefs. But would I be willing to take steps to see to it that that disaster occurs? No. I feel I was deeply wronged by the writer Janet Malcolm in two articles she wrote about me for the *New Yorker* in 1983. I wanted revenge. But the only revenge I felt justified in attempting to inflict was a lawsuit (I lost, but not before a certain vindication before the United States Supreme Court). I never even allowed myself to fantasize hurting Janet Malcolm physically, but merely that on her deathbed she would repent and "confess." I probably have a long wait.

If we can change the laws about animals we will achieve, I believe, far more than if we force, at the point of a gun, or a match, or a threat, vivisectionists to come round to our view. Whatever they might say, they will not do so, certainly not by coercion.

I was shocked the other day to hear Ingrid Newkirk say that Temple Grandin, in working to improve slaughterhouses, had probably done more to relieve animal suffering than any other person alive. Shocked because I do not like the views of Temple Grandin, and I do not believe that somebody who cares about animals will simply improve the conditions of their death, rather than fight to keep them alive and out of harm's way. When we think about it, there is something deeply *psychopathic* – and I use that word infrequently – about raising animals for their flesh and their organs. I don't know if any of you have read the remarkable novel by Kazuo Ishiguro, *Never Let Me Go*, about children raised in what appear to be ordinary boarding schools. Slowly it emerges that they are kept there by other humans for a sinister purpose: the "donation" of their organs. When they have donated for the fourth time, they "complete"; that is, they die, unless they are unfortunate enough to be kept for the use of other parts of their body. The concern is never with their suffering, only with the illnesses of "other," "better" human beings. (There's the single most dangerous idea of the human species: pseudospeciation, the belief that we are superior.) The novel is chilling. The parallel with animals on farms is unavoidable. Or so I thought. But nobody who read the novel saw it that way, and I wonder whether it ever crossed Ishiguro's mind. Among the many discussions on the Internet, nobody mentions what to me is such an obvious comparison. If *you* read the novel, you will immediately agree with me. But that means we are really the minority. *We* are not mainstream.

So I recognize that Ingrid Newkirk may be right, and that it behooves us to allow everyone his or her own methods of persuasion. If Temple Grandin can persuade the owners of slaughterhouses that animals are suffering there unnecessarily, perhaps this is the first little step they need to take toward a deeper vision. I don't think so, but it could be. And even if I am wrong about extreme action, and it is indeed the only way to effect change (and the parallel with slavery is very powerful, and in some ways convincing: do you simply sit in your cozy office and write articles while humans are dying from other people's cruelty?), I have to recognize the limits of my own willingness to act. Perhaps, without realizing it, I too am a member of the mainstream. Maybe it is harder for me to walk away from my liberal education and liberal beliefs when it comes to acts of physical violence than I think. Maybe it has nothing to do with belief, but simply with acculturation. What makes me think I can just walk away from the way I was brought up? Perhaps I can do so in some areas, but not all, and it is possible that precisely this is one of them.

It is possible, but I don't think so, and that is why reading Lee Hall's book has been so important for me. She thinks further than I have thought about certain areas, and I am thrilled to be able to follow her on this extraordinary mental adventure. Buckle up and prepare for the ride of your life!

JEFFREY MOUSSAIEFF MASSON
AUCKLAND, NEW ZEALAND,
MARCH 8, 2006.

Acknowledgments

I thank Edita Birnkrant, Daniel Hammer, and Lisa M. Stanley for their thoughts and ideas about activism and social change, Dan Brook for generous editing advice, and Mark Zuckerman of Circulation Specialists Design for design and production guidance. I'm grateful too for the steadfast encouragement of my co-workers at Friends of Animals and the organization's intrepid supporters, particularly those who participated in the Foundations of a Movement conference in the summer of 2005. Jay Tutchton of the Denver University Law Clinic has provided a model of determined advocacy for the interests of free-living animals. Mark Potok of the Southern Poverty Law Center has been, and continues to be, quintessentially thought-provoking. A number of groups and individuals have offered unique fora to explore threads that became essential to the fabric of this book. They include *Dissident Voice*, the *Ecofem.org Journal*, Rob Eccles, Priscilla Feral, Roz Hendrickson, Chris Kelly, Dan Kowalski of *Bender's Immigration Bulletin*, Loren Lockman, the North American Vegetarian Society, the Animal Law Committee of the New Jersey State Bar Association,

Bob Orabona, Rutgers University at Newark, Lynnette Shanley, SuTao Café, the Unitarian Universalist Congregations of East Brunswick and Somerset Hills, the Earth Ethics Committee of the Washington Ethical Society, the *UCLA Women's Law Review*, and the Vegan Society.

Profound respect and thanks to those of you who have explained, either to me or to my co-workers, that you had considered intimidation both necessary and morally acceptable but changed your minds. I hope you don't mind my lavishing upon you my excess nurturing instincts. Your words have strengthened me and called my attention to a failing of this book, for I know that thoughtfulness, gentleness, and grace – and perhaps even the rejection of utilitarianism – is entirely likely to be found in those whose tactics I'll critique in its chapters. Thank you to anyone who decides, whether prompted by the ideas here or independently of them, to question privilege and subjugation, within or between these forms we call species.

Introduction

E arly in the year 2005, British Home Secretary Charles Clarke declared that an amalgam of new laws, enacted mainly to confront international terrorism, could be used to put Britons themselves under house arrest without criminal trial.[1] Triggered by secret evidence, the measures include attaching electronic tags onto a person, prohibiting somebody's telephone and Internet use, and imposing restrictions on people to whom they're allowed to speak. The Britons targeted by the government belong to the far-right British National Party, and groups promoting animal-welfare militancy.

Eerie as the restrictions might be, eerier still is the public image of animal advocates as adding energy to the mass of threats normally posed by right-wing vigilantes. Underscoring the parallel, Scotland's *Herald* reported in 2005 that animal-rights extremism borrowed a "leaderless resistance" model of activism from the Ku Klux Klan.[2]

British police and intelligence units forged ahead. Working in secret, agents drew up a map of hot spots for violent threats. The map, unveiled at a meeting of the Police Superintendents' Association, was a key factor in a police proposal for sweeping changes to the structure of law enforcement in England and Wales. A news report explained: "The map brings together information about Muslim radicalism, Irish terrorism and activities by animal rights groups."[3]

In the United States, in the summer of 2005, an announcement purportedly from an animal advocacy group named WAR called for letters to be sent to anyone scheduled to speak at a conference which would feature a talk by civil rights advocate Mark Potok.[4] The announcements protested Potok's editorial work for the Southern Poverty Law Center, specifically the quarterly members' magazine, *Intelligence Report*, which had compared the intimidation and destruction used by environmental and animal-welfare militants with the tactics of hate groups.[5] The ominous subtitle: "Radical environmental and animal-rights groups have always drawn the line at targeting humans. Not anymore."

People who work to advance the interests of animals and environmental protection compared with terrorists or hate groups? Surely that was off the mark. But within months of the publication of Southern Poverty Law's report on the rise of animal-welfare militancy, a former South Australian Senate candidate, critical of the conditions on sheep boats destined for middle-eastern countries, admitted contaminating the animals' food with shredded ham.

The press, by this time, was commenting on the parallels between the rhetoric of animal-welfare militants and the actions of fanatical anti-abortionists.[6] The comparison is alarming: North American anti-abortionists have perpetrated seven killings. They've attempted seventeen more. Soon a trauma surgeon named Jerry Vlasak would be quoted in the international press as suggesting that animal liberation would be advanced by the assassinations of five to fifteen experimenters.[7] Vlasak is one of the four spokespeople presently listed on the North American Animal Liberation Press Office website. One of the other three founding spokespeople, Steven Best, offers an essay on the site to explain that Vlasak isn't worried that the negative publicity will discredit animal advocacy – any more than militant acts threatened the anti-abortion movement.

Enough people have been lured by the position of Best and Vlasak to keep the Federal Bureau of Investigation opening cases from coast to coast. Hunting advocacy groups, along with conservative members of Congress, have had a veritable field day, establishing draconian punishments for what they call eco-terrorists. This, although the Animal Enterprise Protection Act of 1992 was already on the books, enacted specifically to catch animal campaigners by outlawing physical disruptions of commercial or academic uses of animals, including laboratories, farms, zoos, aquaria, circuses and other animal shows.

In May 2004, after a three-year investigation that involved the Joint Terrorism Task Force, agents rounded up seven youths accused of connections with attacks on a variety of targets. The investigation had generated the highest number of surveillance authorizations of any case in 2003 – more than 141,000. A grand jury in New Jersey indicted the youths, all affiliated with the group Stop Huntingdon Animal Cruelty, or SHAC, for conspiracy to violate the Animal Enterprise Protection Act, amended in 2002 in a climate of national fear to include "animal enterprise terrorism." The changes made it easier to convict people for attacks on laboratories, in some cases increasing mandatory jail sentences three times over.[8] Three SHAC members were also charged with interstate stalking.

Their campaign target, Huntingdon Life Sciences, has tested drugs, food additives and industrial chemicals for concerns such as BASF, Bayer, Bristol Myers Squibb, British Petroleum, DuPont, Pfizer, Shell, and the Society of the Plastics Industry. Since its beginning in England in 1999, the campaign has attempted to obstruct Huntingdon's interactions with investors and insurers. The U.S. campaign targeted the Bank of New York and a client, a California-based antibiotic producer known as the Chiron Corporation.[9] SHAC's tactics have prompted numerous companies to refuse to work with Huntingdon, and it is only Huntingdon that the campaign means to disable. At least two Huntingdon board members have resigned as a result of the campaign, as has company auditor Deloitte & Touche, the security firm that protects the Huntingdon laboratory, a landscaping contractor and a person who delivers employees' sandwiches.[10]

One of the SHAC campaigners charged in connection with the "multi-pronged attack on the workers, shareholders and clients" of Huntingdon, and using the Internet to incite others to carry out various acts of disruption, is twenty-six year-old Lauren Gazzola. When convicted in early 2006, Gazzola was planning to attend law school. Gazzola ran the U.S. branch of the campaign against Huntingdon ran for several years, after first hearing of the crusade as a teen attending shows by hardcore bands – heavy-metal rock groups with militant animal and earth advocacy themes. "At the time, in the late 1990s, the hardcore scene was very political." Today, Gazzola says, "I'm not really about that anymore."[11]

The indictment against Gazzola and six others quoted the SHAC website, describing vandalism at an insurance director's golf green as having been executed by an Animal Liberation Front "Commando Division." Demonstrations at the homes of employees and their families, including one which Gazzola reportedly attended and where the family was threatened with arson, were described in the grand jury's indictment, and jurors in the ensuing trial watched a videotape of Gazzola protesting in Boston, warning a target, "The police can't protect you!" In the indictment and in the news, bulk e-mails were called "e-mail bombs."[12]

The indictment quoted from the "top 20 terror tactics" – a list which, in addition to listing several innocuous ideas, suggests "physical assault including spraying cleaning fluid into one's eyes" and "threats to kill or injure one's partner or children." Gazzola objects that SHAC campaigners didn't write the list, but had in fact posted it on the Internet with sardonic intent. In the current political climate, this drew an official reaction similar to one that could be caused by bomb jokes at an airport.

Six defendants were convicted of conspiracy to violate Animal Enterprise Protection Act. Here are examples of incidents listed in that charge, specifically involving the Chiron Corporation:

*70. On or about May 16, 2003, the SHAC Website posted a report
of the demonstration at the home of AH stating: Very early this
morning C[. Corp.] employees and board members woke up to the
sounds of activists screaming though bullhorns, personal alarms
blaring in the front yards and to find flyers with their pictures,
names and addresses posted up around their neighborhoods exposing the sick animal killing scum that they are.*

*71. On or about August 18, 2003, individuals went to the home of AH
and, pounded on her front door, rang her doorbell and shouting
"open the door you fucking bitch."[13]*

SHAC supporters view the conspiracy convictions of six of the seven computer users as a bizarre affront to people who report and distribute news. Many observers see the case as a test of free speech law in an electronic age. It was 1969, in the case of *Brandenburg v. Ohio*, that the U.S. Supreme Court held that a speaker could not be punished for advocating illegal action unless the speech is (1) directed at producing imminent lawless conduct, and (2) likely to result in such conduct. SHAC's prosecutors insisted that freedom-of-speech protections did not apply to the young campaigners, for they had crossed the line from civil demonstration to domestic terrorism in a "conspiracy of terror" to incite followers to cause physical and emotional harm.[14]

Big money was at stake. Huntingdon's stock became unavailable for purchase by many institutional investors and hedge funds when stock trader Stephan "Skip" Boruchin was forced, in early 2006, to drop the company. The media focused on incendiary devices and a hammer hurled through Boruchin's office window. Although threats of continued hammers and the smoke bombs scared people away from doing business with Huntingdon, these threats set back the effort to cultivate a broad understanding of animal rights, for, although "animal rights" was mentioned in the media accounts, readers could not be expected to glean any idea about what respecting animals would actually involve. And the SHAC campaigners, apparently, didn't care. Stop Huntingdon Animal Cruelty's success is measured not by how many members of the public learn about animal interests, or what animal rights would mean in their daily lives. It's measured simply by how many people are deterred from associating with a single company. In those terms, scaring off the people who lend administrative support to Boruchin was a big win. Boruchin's company, Legacy Trading, was known as the only firm consistently facilitating a market in Huntingdon's stock above the level of the volatile Pink Sheet trading, which many investors won't touch.[15]

One journalist, who must have thought that respecting animals has something to do with bird baths, wrote, "Skip Boruchin has nothing against animals. He gives his pet bird, which has a skin condition, a special chemical bath so its feathers won't fall off."[16] The campaigners did communicate with Boruchin; but not so much with an educational purpose as with a conviction that Boruchin's office was a stop on the way – or in the way – to the next campaign goal.

"I consider everybody whom I've come into contact with from SHAC to be very bright," Boruchin said in an interview for the electronic magazine *Salon.com*. "Initially, they're like anybody else – you get more done with carrots than sticks. But their soft, nice approach lasted about 20 minutes. And then it's, 'Look at the actions we've taken. Look at what we've done to other people. Look at our Web site.'" Thereafter, according to Boruchin, the calls went: "Fucking puppy killer! [click]"

"Six Animal Rights Advocates Are Convicted of Terrorism" announced the *New York Times* on the third day of March, 2006 – ensuring that many more people have now heard the term "animal rights" in connection with people who can and will resort to coercive acts within twenty minutes. Most of those readers are unlikely to ever meet people who think seriously about respecting animals. And people think seriously not because someone hangs out a neon sign welcoming violent ideology, but because they decide to follow an intuitive pull, a desire to act ethically. To live meaningful, thoughtful lives. The matter for this book to explore, then, is why some segments of animal advocacy have become increasingly willing to dispense in twenty minutes with a respectful approach.

For individual campaigners, the consequences are unquestionably harsh. Between the SHAC trial and two other recent sets of grand jury indictments in the western states – a string of sabotage activities in Oregon, California, and Wyoming; a firebombing that caused $12 million in damage at a Colorado ski resort – the people known in the newspapers as "environmental and animal rights activists" face severe sentences, and, in some cases, severe pressure amongst themselves, due to the conflicts between their personal legal interests and the interests of other suspects. Many defendants were still in their teens when they gravitated to militancy, and now they must choose between following the advice of their lawyers or that of their peers. Their families face social pressure, loss and anguish, not to mention the task of finding enormous amounts of money for lawyers and bail. Supportive Internet sites built by families may maintain a defendant's innocence when, at the same time, peers are posting tributes to the defendant's proven devotion to the militant cause.

The aftermath of any conviction invariably includes a flurry of competition to inject opinion into the media. Upon hearing the news of the convictions in the New Jersey SHAC trial, opponents of activism such as Americans for Medical Progress warned that the verdict would trigger more violence, and called on federal lawmakers to strengthen the laws.[17] SHAC's reaction appeared to be custom-tailored to its opponents: Pamelyn Ferdin, the current president of SHAC USA, declared, "People, I think, are going to get hurt. There's going to be a lot of violence."[18]

And the militants' targets are often people who happen to be in the wrong place at the wrong time – or, one suspects, so they must feel. It was late 2004 when someone broke into Seaboard Securities, a Florida brokerage firm. Left in the office were damaged computers, markings with the initials of the Animal Liberation Front, and a note that warned "Drop HLSI" – presumably a reference to Seaboard's connections with Huntingdon Life Sciences. The next day, police reports state, a group of masked people with signs rushed into the company's Juno Beach branch, knocking one employee in the head with a bullhorn and throwing a potted poinsettia.[19] Three twenty-something-year-old people subsequently faced charges of criminal mischief, burglary, and wearing masks during a crime.

After the two incidents, Seaboard Securities, like Skip Boruchin, reportedly stopped dealing with Huntingdon stocks. And that was the point of the foray. The surface success of these incidents is deceptive, however, because a reduction in experiments is not in sight as long as governments require toxicity testing on nonhuman subjects for each new drug that enters the market. The constant development and marketing of new drugs, chemicals, and procedures keeps thousands of testing labs in business, apart from Huntingdon's three sites. Meanwhile, prison companies stand to benefit every time some twenty-something-year-old kid stands in court. One of the people charged in the Florida incident, according to court documents, told police of having received instructions about the protest via e-mail from New York – a sequence which, in today's political climate, gives authorities fuel to contemplate restrictions on private computer use. If all of that doesn't paint a dire enough picture, consider an entire community learning to associate animal advocacy with physical altercations and the ridiculous scene of a potted plant heaved through a roomful of hapless clerks.

Things are getting stranger still. Campaigners in England have targeted a pharmaceutical agent who has been dead for more than a year.[20] The family of the late Alexander Grant was at home on the October day their car was set afire; the Internet site of the militant publication *Bite Back* later announced that "your decisions will come back to haunt you forever even when you have gone." Grant was a senior director of Roche, a company that has contracts with Huntingdon Life Sciences. And that fire comes just weeks after a chain of children's nurseries was targeted. The directors of Leapfrog Day Nurseries, Britain's biggest childcare provider, received letters warning them to stop offering services to Huntingdon employees. They stopped. A spokesperson for the nursery firm responded, "Our business is childcare and we have to take every precaution when it comes to the security and safety of those children and our employees."[21]

The letter to Leapfrog claimed to come from the Animal Rights Militia – a group established in 1985 to promote military-style tactics at a time when the Animal Liberation Front held fast to pacifist principles. The Militia's letter stated:

> *The company you work for is working with Huntingdon Life Sciences. This is a disgusting and cowardly act. You have a choice. You can walk away from those sick monsters or you can personally face the consequences of your decision. Not only you but your family is a target. Sever your links with HLS within two weeks or get ready for your life and the lives of those you love to become a living hell.*[22]

By late 2005, leading members of Britain's pharmaceutical industry were calling for more restrictions on the movements of animal-welfare militants, including bans on international travel. And such ideas are no longer far-fetched.[23] Threats and intimidation, however spruced up with terms like "direct action," can turn the community against activists and cause people to stand aside for law enforcement to do as it will.

This book will not just provide a chronicle or and analysis of events, although it will do that. This book will not talk about distinguishing pragmatic action from counterproductive activities, although it will do that too. This book will not talk only about the significance of civil liberties and the enormous public interests served when a society has the strength to respect critique, dissent, and protest. It will do that. But most important, this book will take an ethical stand: Animal rights, in its theory and its practice, provides a model for people who seek activism as integrity. Thus, there is no confusion between its end and its means; it doesn't throw away its moral standards in the short term and claim that doing so will result in some later moral pay-off. It doesn't seek martyrs. It is not based on deterring, incapacitating, or visiting retribution on some opponent. It says, simply, that deliberately sowing fear is never justified. And those who sow it cannot address the root causes of animal use, even when those causes could be readily and effectively addressed.

Considering one more example will expand that last point. Jersey Cuts, a New Jersey meatpacker, closed in the summer of 1999 after a second firebombing by militants. This attack on the company's economic interest resulted in a meaningless victory, for it had no bearing on shoppers' interest in meat. Changing corporate activity is something that we all have the power to do, not by making firebombs, but simply by withholding money. Granted, this is harder to accomplish as large multinationals take over more and more of the food supply – but that's part of what effective activists must address. We change the make-up of food businesses through the day-to-day decisions about what food we will eat.

Indeed, food is so central to our society that our attitudes about it are likely to influence everything we do. A fundamental change in the way humans view other animals must begin with food…not bombs; for there is simply no good reason to accept the conception of revolution as inherently violent or destructive. When violence and destruction has, for century after century, been the tedious norm, non-violence is revolutionary.

PART ONE

THE AVENGERS

CHAPTER ONE

Do not confuse motion and progress.
A rocking horse keeps moving,
but does not make any progress.

ALFRED A. MONTAPERT

A Sheen of Respectability?

David Martosko, as research director for the non-profit Center for Consumer Freedom, claims to speak for certain restaurant and food industry actors.[1] In May 2005, Martosko appeared before the U.S. Senate's Environment and Public Works Committee, telling the lawmakers about the "sheen of respectability" gained by the most militant supporters of the Animal Liberation Front and Earth Liberation Front through the efforts of Steven Best.[2] Best teaches philosophy, and co-founded the North American Animal Liberation Press Office, the Web-based platform for communicating actions and strategies for ensuring the welfare of animals.

To Martosko and similar critics, Steven Best is a godsend. How odd that an animal advocate would offer the type of ammunition seen, for example, in Best's recent essay "My Dog or Your Child? Ethical Dilemmas and the Hierarchy of Moral Value."

"Too often," begins Best, "animal rights advocates are challenged with the hysterical hypothetical of the 'burning house dilemma'." If one were escaping a burning house with time to save either a human or some other animal, goes the question, which would one save?" (I've never been challenged with that one during my two decades of animal rights advocacy; I've only heard it discussed by academic writers. But who knows. Maybe some activists wear badges on their lapels that say "Ask me about the burning house.") "If the dog is my dog and the human is a total stranger to me," Best decides, "I will in every case save my dog." Best doesn't stop there, but instead seizes the occasion to taunt readers for any "irrational allegiance to a species as demented, troubled, and undeserving as *Homo sapiens*" and declares:

> *To be frank, I would save my own dog over 1, 10, oh, I don't know how many human strangers, especially if they were vile animal abusers... Let the speciesists bitch and bray, reader; just be glad that you are not their dog or cat, for they would sell you out to a lousy biped in a heartbeat.*

Applying the choice question to a conflict between the interests of a harp seal and a hunter, Best persists in the same inflammatory mode:

> *Not only would I save the seal from the barbarian who makes his living clubbing such beautiful pups over the head and skinning them alive, I would save the seal over a billion bastards like him. Similarly, I would send an infinite number of Ted Nugent cretins over a steep cliff to save a deer, elk, bear, or any other animal they kill for pleasure. I'd do it to save a cockroach, a flea, or a tick. Or a blade of grass. The planet is a better place without sadists who kill animals for pleasure or profit.*

Quoting liberally from utilitarian philosopher Peter Singer, Best views cats, dogs, dolphins, and chimpanzees as persons, as opposed to non-persons. The non-persons are human infants, the severely brain-impaired, the comatose, and those in the advanced stages of Alzheimer's. Best next declares that a chimpanzee is "smarter than a three or four year old child," so "[f]rom a non-speciesist ethical perspective, it is the right thing" to confine human infants in cages for AIDS research instead; Best adds that the data would be better. Otherwise, Best says, one ought to renounce all such testing. Without going into any details about what the non-speciesists would do with caged children who live past four, Best proceeds to declare a preference for "my dog over my brain dead mother, a dolphin over a cat, and a chimpanzee over a dog", and ends up giving even the non-sadistic human a decidedly low place on the wish list, asking, "Is not a happy dog preferable to a miserable human being whose consumer lifestyle is a burden on the planet?"

Then, Best says that the hypothetical choices present false dilemmas anyway. Animal advocates, says Best, "emphasize that there are few bona fide cases where human and animal interests might conflict…" To the extent that it agrees with such advocates, Best's argument fails, as one can see from any overview of environmental case law, or a study of responses to disasters. Recall, for instance, the heart-wrenching scenes of evacuation authorities separating humans from pets in the wreckage of Hurricane Katrina. Or look at the nearest road works project, where birds and mice and feral cats are routinely moved from nest, bush and burrow.[3]

Oddly enough, Best claims to extend Martin Luther King's ideology to animal rights, and in the very next paragraph calls a detractor, whose name is Brian O'Connor, "Herr O'Connor" and "Brain Dead O'Connor," and "senile." O'Connor has decided that Steven Best displays "the self-indulgence of the egocentric masquerading as a lofty moral principle." Best's response? "Move over Ward Churchill, you have company." And indeed, a Ward Churchill foreword appears in Steven Best's co-edited book, *Terrorists or Freedom Fighters?*

Whatever merits or shortfalls might exist in the ample body of Ward Churchill's scholarship, the University of Colorado professor is now, and might forever be, best known for an essay that referred to the dead of 11 September as "Little Eichmanns" who were "self-importantly braying on their cell phones" when disaster struck. Social critic Michael Albert gives a particularly sensitive account of the essay's effect:

My reaction was to wish he hadn't written it. Ward took clear and cogent insights about the causes of international hostility to U.S. policies and weighed them down with not so clear and not so cogent non insights about the general population of the U.S. This kind of mix is always a problem, not least because astute but reactionary readers will try to dismiss the good by pointing to the bad.[4]

Albert rightly warns progressive people not to dismiss or attack the writer's person when the focus ought to be on that writer's substantive work. But then, that's precisely the difficulty facing the reader when a political critique crosses that line between the stunningly provocative and the blindingly immoderate.

Ward Churchill is not the only personality to wield a Nazi reference like a blunt instrument to find the general population guilty; the tactic is also used by Best. An anti-meat exhibit called *Holocaust on Your Plate* gets high marks from Best for "most judiciously" comparing the situation of animals in factory farms with Jews killed by Nazis. In Steven Best's model, the provocation upstages the message. "I adopt an earth-centered perspective ('biocentrism') over a human-centered perspective ('anthropocentrism')," proclaims Best, "such that I view the needs of the earth and biodiversity to be more important than the life of any single human being, myself included." Best then takes "My Dog or Your Child? Ethical Dilemmas and the Hierarchy of Moral Value" to its grandstanding peak:

I would rather the regeneration of the earth transpire than have humans continue to devour and destroy the planet with their SUVs, superhighways, urban sprawl, cookie-cutter suburbs, bloated families, fast food addictions, Supersize Me appetites, arrogance and alienation, and grotesque fat asses.

Best concludes with a section called Ponder Thy Plate, which suggests vegetarianism as a sound ethical commitment. Many environmentalists, social justice activists, and animal advocates have made similar suggestions without feeling obliged to lead up to it with several hundred words of irritating bluster.

Best's bluster, too, is hardly original; it seems a deliberate revival of the manner adopted by Paul Watson, who has been associated with animal protection and environmental activism for more than three decades and claims to have invented tree-spiking. That tactic, which entails hammering metal stakes into trees to deter timber workers from sawing, is outlawed in numerous states. Not surprising. Spiking doesn't harm a tree, but it can shatter a chain saw, and in 1987 a timber worker was seriously injured by a saw that broke apart on a spike. In the same year, a sawmill blade struck a tree spike at the Louisiana Pacific mill in Cloverdale, California, sending metal shards across the room and breaking a worker's jaw.[5]

The environmental activist Judi Bari and Oregon mill worker Gene Lawhorn made it clear, at the 1990 gathering known as Redwood Summer, that tree-spiking was dangerous, and patently out of place in ethical environmentalism. Paul Watson, writing in the *Earth First! Journal* later that year, excoriated Bari for creating an alliance with workers, for "it was with both pride and satisfaction" that Watson "relished the reports of tree-spiking" in the environmental movement. Spiking "generates discussion in the media" and by using it, Watson added, "forest defenders could keep the industry and their lackey workers on the defensive."[6]

Bari, said Watson, "is acting from an anthropocentric ethical foundation and I am coming from a biocentric base." In reality, Bari had always maintained a biocentric grounding. It was clearly Bari's alliance with the mill workers that drew Watson's ire: "There was a weak link in our movement. Those anthropocentric, socialistic types – whose hearts bleed for the antiquated rights of the workers – were won over."

Bari was no weak link. Bari was an expansive thinker and organizer who knew that the pillaging of forests is part of a larger problem in which social inequities can easily combine with disregard for the environment. Watson, in contrast, chose to see the workers as "a rot, a disease and an aberration against nature," and "pathetic foot-soldiers to the corporate generals of the logging industry." Ignoring the history of Pacific Lumber, whose employees were forced out of an environmentally responsible company after a corporate raid, Watson sniffed, "Certainly they are being exploited by the companies, but they have made the decision to be exploited." Watson concludes with a declaration that "tree-spiking will continue. ...despite the laws of society, despite the so-called 'rights' of the loggers and their ilk."

Those who take a militant view of environmental and animal advocacy frequently brush rights aside in order to argue that ends justify means. Watson has more recently stated, "I personally cannot get overly worked up about deprivation of human rights in a world where non-humans have no rights at all."[7] Watson liberally splashes "not so cogent non insights about the general population" on environmentalist concepts by defining humanity as "the last of the hominid primates, and this was a group that was never very successful to begin with – overly territorial, obsessed with trivialities, violent, petty, and completely lacking in empathy for other species." Watson adds: "The world will be a much nicer place without us." Flirting with outright misanthropy, Watson professes to have "dropped any pretension of loyalty to humankind."[8]

Like Watson's rhetoric, Steven Best's "grotesque fat asses" manifesto appeals to activists looking for community or catharsis. It's apparent, judging by the acceptance this rhetoric has found in some circles, that a function is served by figures who appeal to the perennial frustration and powerlessness of youth, who can repackage a philosophy to allow for, or even glorify, a span of attention stunted by high-fructose corn syrup and Bruce Willis films. This kind of thing is very successful in sending crops of people in their teens and twenties into the arms of prosecutors every season. Whether activists actually succeed in changing societal attitudes is another matter. Mark Potok, the speaker from the Southern Poverty Law Center, has referred to bombastic and showy activism as "swashbuckling." Where the word fits, it raises the question of whether some high-profile animal advocates are using the idea of animals' vulnerability to forge their identities – surely as instrumental a use of animals as any other.

And to the extent that such advocates or their protégés believe that they will control situations through force, unpredictable tactics, and dangerous devices, who will trust them? Who – human or not; willing and able to fight or not – could rely upon them to act with the respect and integrity necessary to lead the expansion of humanity's moral community? If they believe deliberate intimidation is acceptable or virtuous, then they believe, even if not consciously or intentionally, in establishing hierarchy. They would be at a loss without it.

But it's too simple to wave them off and say, well they never did subscribe to rights-based principles, they really have nothing to do with animal rights; now let's forget about them and get our work done. To address and unravel this mental dynamic takes more attention. People understandably think it difficult to learn what we mean by an animal-rights movement as something separate from the mass of contradictory statements and campaigns "for the animals." It's not easy for the public to hear anything above that cacophonous din that today passes for activism. Swashbuckling is one of the most effective silencers of the ethically consistent activist's voice.

CHAPTER TWO

To an ordinary human being,
love means nothing if it does not mean loving
some people more than others.

GEORGE ORWELL

The Vegetarian Lifeboat

Animal equality theorists sometimes pose a hypothetical us-or-them emergency. If one were escaping a burning house with time to save either a human or some other animal, goes the question, which would one save? If a lifeboat could only continue to float when the weight of one of its occupants – human or dog – were thrown overboard, who should be tossed out to drown?

In philosopher Tom Regan's lifeboat scenario, four humans and a dog need the lifeboat; but there is not enough room for all, so one must drown. Regan sees the humans and the dog as equally morally significant in that all qualify as "subjects-of-a-life," a moral status drawing equal consideration for basic rights. Yet Regan finds it morally appropriate to let the dog die, as "no reasonable person would deny that the death of any of the four humans would be a greater...harm" than the dog's death would be.[1]

Some scholars answer the lifeboat question at great length, supplying many detailed variations. But usually, as Regan does, they answer that the human, being human, gets priority in most cases, or that the human, being human, could get automatic priority and that wouldn't invalidate the animal advocate's position. That is, a moral loophole would be an acceptable part of the theoretical fabric, given that there are so few burning houses and sinking lifeboats containing both humans and dogs.

While all those discussions about the hypothetical fire and lifeboat were being written, a rather large heat- and water-related emergency has arisen. This emergency involves global climate patterns which are exacerbating weather changes worldwide. Writers are paying increasing attention to the dire circumstances already faced by residents of icy or sea-level regions. Polar bears are losing their moorings and drowning in open seas; Dutch workers are constructing buoyant roads and amphibious homes.[2]

Researchers commissioned by the Pentagon – their names are Peter Schwartz and Doug Randall – wrote a report that "suggests that because of the potentially dire consequences, the risk of abrupt climate change, although uncertain and quite possibly small, should be elevated beyond a scientific debate to a U.S. national security concern."[3] In the near future, Schwartz and Randall state, "it is not implausible that abrupt climate change will bring extreme weather conditions to many of the world's key population and growing regions at the same time – stressing global food, water, and energy supply." Bangladesh, for example, could be made nearly uninhabitable by persistent typhoons and coastal floods. Conflict over basic needs could turn Europe and the United States into fully guarded zones, with security personnel staving off millions of migrants.

A fair response to such developments would be different: The wealthier regions would prepare to take responsibility for assisting the evacuated people to the best of their ability to do so. Surely we have a moral duty to assist another who faces a peril that we have done so much to create: The United States is the largest emitter of carbon in the world. To put this into context, although the U.S. population makes up only about five per cent of humanity, it's the source of about a quarter of the world's extra carbon emissions, the average resident putting out about 100 times the carbon created by the average Bangladeshi.[4]

A key feature of the U.S. lifestyle is its appetite. All those hamburgers and the process of making them are, to the environmentally aware, notorious for releasing warming gas into the air. We normally hear about excess carbon dioxide, and the disappearance of the forests which absorb it. There's a lot of hand-wringing and talk about if or when the politicians are going to do something. But do we hear that agribusiness is the prime culprit behind the loss of forests, and that *we can do something to stop it today?* The methane that accounts for nine percent of all U.S. greenhouse gas emissions, and which has more than twenty times the warming potential of carbon dioxide, is generated during cows' digestion processes, as well as by the consumption of oil and gas in animal processing.[5]

When is it time to total the losses to the earth when lands are made over to grazing and the raising of feed? When will environmentalists make it known, not just to the choir but in their public alerts and releases, that behind virtually every great environmental complaint there's milk and meat? The environmental journalist and social critic George Monbiot has noted that meat and dairy animals (that's just the big animals) already outnumber their owners around the world three-to-one – meaning that the space and resources involved in meat and dairy enterprises are enormous – and that the resultant products are largely shuttled to the world's most affluent populations.

In the United States, beef vendors are the hardy beneficiaries of a perennial masculine appeal. Burgers should weigh a quarter-pound; roast beef isn't acceptable in thin European slices, but must come to the table in heaps. The package cover of Swanson's "XXL" Angus Meat Loaf dinner hawks "1½-pounds of food," and the brand's Hungry-Man All-Day Breakfast promises the buyer satisfaction in the form of 64 grams of fat, 2,090 milligrams of sodium, and 231% of the all-day cholesterol limit.

In tribute to the corporate heads' XXL bank accounts, cows are sacrificed at the rate of some 100,000 every day. That's just cows: a hundred thousand every day. So that public lands might become private feedlots, U.S. government agents have busied themselves year after year with projects that have burnt, shot, trapped, and poisoned the land's indigenous animals. Some 56 million acres of U.S. territory are stripped of oxygen-giving trees, and then used to produce hay for animals bred to be food; only four million acres produce vegetables for direct human consumption.[6] The hay is not necessary. The vegetables are.

The British government's Chief Scientist, David King, has called global warming a greater threat than terrorism. So has Hans Blix, who headed the United Nations weapons inspections in Iraq. It's not just the security of human nations but the security of terrestrial life at risk. Emergencies shouldn't guide ethics, but it's surely worth taking note when all life on earth may indeed be clinging to a lifeboat, with the world's wealthiest humans consuming like there's no tomorrow and tossing everyone else over the sides.[7]

Instead of taking note, most animal advocacy deals with symptoms, including the constant need to rescue individual animals, without making the root causes of that need clear – that is, without ever challenging the presumption that we may make other animals over to us wherever we perceive it will bring us advantages or pleasures. One rationale for doing so is the assertion that we confer a benefit upon animals, no matter what our purpose might be for doing so, simply by breeding them into existence. An intensified form of that rationale is that treating them mercifully mitigates our use of them. So these days, in collaboration with modern, international grocers, many advocates are calling for a return to raising animals the old-fashioned way, on family farms.

We'll come back to the rescue concept. The free-range farming issue can be dispensed with at once. U.S. corporations annually process billions of chickens and fish, over 100 million pigs, and tens of millions of cattle, calves, sheep and lambs. In order to provide true freedom of movement for the cattle and sheep and chickens, we'd have to clear any remaining national parks and forests, and then invade several more countries.

Free-range farming still relies on bringing animals into life as commodities, it usurps trees and water and the habitat that free-living animals need to enjoy what's really the only animal right in the world – their privacy from our intrusions. Free-range farms do not solve the problem of methane gas associated with ruminant animals. And the free-range label persuades some shoppers who see factory farms as inhumane, uncouth, or biologically dangerous to buy animal products.

For investors in this sector, profits can be impressive. By 2006, the value of non-cage egg sales in Britain was ahead of the value of cage-produced eggs. But the cage-free label doesn't guarantee any minimum space, or access to the outdoors. Most purportedly "free-range" offerings are, in reality, mass-produced commodities involving no pastures at all. The egg and dairy industries are notorious for their overall treatment, and the few cast-offs living in sanctuaries were typically found starved, neglected or abused – common situations for animals raised for human consumption, including on so-called family farms.

Co-incidently, those who can afford to purchase goods from today's old-fashioned farms are also able to donate liberally to charity. Today, well-meaning people say that buying products marked with a free-range label is the equivalent of a charitable donation, and restaurateurs who sell purportedly compassionate meat dishes donate generously to humane causes. Thus, the donor who cheers animal rescue groups might be the same person who eats the animals from today's family farm. In other words, they may pay to rescue and to consume animals from the same industry. There's one reason for this dissonance: Most of professionalized advocacy avoids taking seriously the point that animals are conscious beings and not mere things. They don't encourage their members to be vegetarians; they encourage them to buy animal products from preferred producers.[8] The position of professionalized advocacy today, for all its millions in wealth, has largely reduced itself to a gatekeeper function, a role of certifying that this or that company's cages are not the smallest, that the killing floors are not the most crowded or staffed by the least trained people. After all, the sprawling welfare administrations could never apply consumer pressure to multinational animal agribusinesses, or make high-profile agreements and expand their sphere of influence and grow their millions in various banks, if their members were vegetarians.

CHAPTER THREE

A transformation that would remain in the same mode of thought, a transformation that would only be a certain way of better adjusting the same thought to the reality of things, would only be a superficial transformation. On the other hand, as soon as people have trouble thinking things the way they have always been thought, transformation becomes at the same time very urgent, very difficult, and entirely possible.

MICHEL FOUCAULT

It's About Us

Animal rights is about animals; but as for the evolution of its theory and practice, it's about us.

Do activists seek a world in which respect prevails, in which love without coercion is possible? Do we see the life that grounds us, that supports us, that runs through our veins, that's connected with every tree, every animal, and do we promise never to harm anything connected with that great and delicate force? As a friend who runs a local Asian vegetarian restaurant has asked me:

The life force is like a mother, it's our parent; and knowing that we all support it by our being, could we ever set out to destroy? How we treat the force that creates us is how we treat our parents. How can you say you believe in it if you don't know how to support it?

To agree with animal rights means, at essence, to repudiate violence, and to transcend the habit of seeing others as instruments to our ends, of taking advantage. It's the refusal to use intimidation. It's the end of tactical force. But, says the reader of the latest militant website, magazine, or book, *What about the intervention in the Second World War? You would not be against that, would you?* Sometimes, pressing the point, the activist will compare humanity's use of other animals with the horror of Nazi concentration camps.

Notwithstanding the claim that forcible action may sometimes be imposed upon the ethical person, people of the world do not see animal commodification as they view the Holocaust. Nor is the comparison likely to move us forward. People understand the Holocaust as an aberration. Barbaric, hideous, unspeakable, unthinkable, grotesque, and immoral by global norms. And rightly so. Yet notice that Germany's commitment to send large numbers of soldiers to their deaths in war was not understood as similarly immoral. Hitler's war caused the deaths of about 40 million people. And yet, if not for the Holocaust, history would have judged Hitler as a failed conqueror rather than a mass-murderer.[1]

By international agreement on what is grotesque, we know what war crimes are. But this assumes, or even purposefully perpetuates the idea, that war itself, a mass filicide whereby a national leader sends streams of young people to their deaths over the human creation called a nation, is *not* a crime against humanity.[2] No one is allowed to raise a fuss over the conventional view that war is a necessary institution, and that individual lives should regularly or gloriously be sacrificed for the health of the body politic. Reversing the menace of war itself is a radical proposition. It is not a matter of refining war's rules. It involves committing ourselves to peace.

By examining the Holocaust and examining war, we find that animal commodification is less like the Holocaust than it is like war. The systematic use of animals throughout the world is seen as normal and natural and inevitable and vaguely eternal, and its only antidote is peace. As long as it goes on, people will decry whatever they deem aberrations, and countries with the time and resources to think about such things will enact anti-cruelty statutes or administrative rules to assuage people's moral concerns and keep moving the whole thing along as usual. When animal-welfare groups focus on the horrendous, the cruel, and the barbaric, they aren't attending to the underlying problem of domination; and in some sense they are ensuring that the everyday domination continues unnoticed.

Animal-rights advocates, along with most of the public, are deeply upset by reports of terrible abuse in situations where animals are used – somebody punching a dog or slinging a monkey by the arm, deriding animals, or leaving them in severe pain. When undercover footage from a Huntingdon lab aired in 1997 on British television, authorities investigated, two technicians pleaded guilty to cruelty to dogs in a case unprecedented in the history of the British testing industry, and the Home Office attached conditions to the laboratory's certification.[3] Similarly, in 1998, an investigation prompted by undercover footage of severe mistreatment of monkeys in Huntingdon's New Jersey lab led the U.S. Department of Agriculture to fine the company $50,000 under the Animal Welfare Act, including for failure to use appropriate anaesthetics or sedatives. Most commentators, while condemning the abuses revealed on videotape, spoke in terms of finding ways to take corrective action in the lab so these abuses would not happen again. There ought to be a law against punching puppies, most people would think – and so there is.

But law or no law, the abuses in Huntingdon's lab, while possibly the most well-known and discussed, should not be considered unusual. Nearly all animals used in labs, even in those labs where husbandry standards are carefully followed, are used insofar as they serve the experimental purpose, and then killed. And if we believe we ought to wield life or death power over other animals, then we can talk about animal welfare and we can make and amend laws infinitely, but what's important to understand is that when we consider them ours to use, inevitably many other degrading abuses will follow.

It is naïve, then, to think of Huntingdon as a special case. To do so sets up confusion: Are activists upset because the activity in this particular lab went out of bounds? If so, then the public will believe the thing to do is to ensure that the lab conforms to husbandry rules. Those rules are in place. All that needs to be done is to enforce them. Get the technician or the lab to clean up its act. Look to the welfare regulations for the minimum standards; make sure that labs and their employees are held responsible for their actions.

But part of lab employment means handling animals as instruments. To consider such animals as individuals with feelings and interests of their own does not facilitate lab work. The very nature of laboratory use means objectifying these animals, thinking of them as foreign to our moral community. Little wonder that abuses take place. It is naïve to think they won't.

Saving animals from the very worst circumstances is the leading paradigm in animal advocacy – both in its militant segments, and in large, donor-driven welfare societies. This model leads to a cyclical position, steering us away from building the necessary fundamental platform for understanding the best role of the activist. By doing the day-to-day work of transcending the culture of dominion, we question the very existence of the institutions that, once formed, render all the shocking aberrations possible.

The trouble with saying this in the activist community is that it's hard for people to grip, when they feel it's urgent to rescue animals who are alive and suffering this instant. And the usual tendency, when wondering where on earth to start advocating, is to focus on the very worst.

The sense of genuine anguish arises in the here and now, and with it, the urge to do something. The feeling is at once immediate and continuous, and it's tied into all the pain that I, the individual, have unwittingly caused. And for an animal belonging to some company or institution, I am always too late, and there is never a recourse to authority. The apes, once subjected to training, can't be sent back to freedom; the cows can't be let loose to enjoy their ecological birthright; nor can the dogs be wolves. The loss happened before we were born; our visions of rescue are illusory.

And we are not warriors. Although animal use, like war, comes packaged as an eternal violence, a natural, regulated, and therefore socially permissible violence, advocates are not obliged to consider the animal rights movement a war, with all the good-and-evil rhetoric that perspective absorbs. Copying the activity of warmakers or soldiers, forcing people to behave or not to behave in certain ways – this perpetuates the paradigm of daily social control by some authoritative force. Other people are not the enemy of animal rights; if there is an enemy at all, it is the tendency to depersonalize others. Using conscious animals as means to an end means depersonalizing them. It involves alienating some individuals, some population, from our moral community, so that we can pull from them what we want. Militancy reinforces precisely the same social habit. Calling someone's home and screaming "Fucking bitch!" means we have decided that, in certain circumstances, there is no need to respect this party's interests or feelings. When a particular objective is at stake, then insofar as the other fails to act according to our wishes, to produce what we want, that party's interests – the other's personhood – means nothing at all.

As no one is free from species bias, there can be no Them. We have all been beneficiaries of the use of animals, the caller and the person who answers the telephone. The caller's anger, then, must to some degree be directed against the self, for both of them, and we too, are part of the class entitled by the law of *Homo sapiens* to own other animals. We might not think about it this way, but we define humanity as the owning class. No matter what comes of our discussions about how to view our relationship with the rest of the biocommunity, it's always about us.

Sixty years after co-founding the Vegan Society, Donald Watson was asked, "What are your views on direct action?" The advocate answered, "If I were an animal in a vivisection cage, I would thank the person who broke in and let me out but, having said that, we must always remember: is it just possible that our act could be counterproductive?"[4]

Watson, a carpenter and woodworking teacher, will be remembered most of all as an educator. (On the occasion of Watson's obituary, the British Broadcasting Company used the term "guru of veganism.") Notably, Watson questioned the wisdom of a rescue – typically considered the most benign form of "direct action" for animals. Watson did not elaborate on what might be counterproductive, but it is not difficult to imagine a rescue as having a counterproductive effect overall. Educating about a vegan life engages the animal-rights question at its fundamental level, whereas rescue is done on personal impulse, and makes no impact on the system that will replace the rescued animal with another.[5] So although private acts of rescue and charity are, from time to time, needed or laudable, it's important to keep in mind that our acts of charity help to offset the results of unfairness, the symptoms of unfairness, as they appear in individual lives. What our charitable actions don't do is interrogate the systemic problem of unfair treatment. Thus the value of being aware, as we work, that charity is often cyclical and symbiotic with the imbalance it seeks to ameliorate. And this is why it is too simple to say, as many advocates do, that rescuing and working for welfare improvements does something for animals here and now, whereas sitting around and critiquing is a luxury.

On the surface it may sound cavalier to respond to a caring person by saying that those animals who are already domesticated or commodified are as out of the reach of rescue as those animals who died last year, or a hundred years ago. Or adding that if they have to be rescued, they will always be dependent beings for whom the concept of animal rights is a platitude. Yet this view is anything but cavalier. Sister Helen Prejean, whose efforts on behalf of death row inmates inspired the film *Dead Man Walking,* was not cavalier to say, about humans who would face capital punishment, "I tell myself that I had simply better accept the fact that the death penalty is here to stay in our society, at least for a while, and there is nothing I can do about it." Prejean added: "Maybe, in time – after how many executions? – people will come to realize the futility of randomly selecting a few people to die each year."

Helen Prejean has performed many individual charitable acts, and surely would not belittle any acts of kindness in prison. But Prejean does not make agreements with the prison-industrial complex, or give advice on how to kill prisoners, or act as an undercover reformist. Prejean has, instead, kept the focus on educating about the need to abolish the injustice that puts all of the individual cases in a common context. The concern, the goal, is not to make capital punishment seem less harsh; it's to end the killing of some human beings by others.

For those who believe that the unnecessary killing of other conscious beings is capricious as well, and perceive their inability to stop it, there is no end, at least for a while, to the procession of calves up the turnpike, the floating thoughts of a hundred thousand faces at night. For many years, their bells tolled to satisfy our own appetites each time we sat down to dinner. And most people around us live just the way we were raised to live. Our culture, traditions, and personal memories resist a commitment to stop consuming other animals. And that is why asking what we would have done to address concentration camps is not the best starting point to persuade a large segment of the public that the animal-rights question is an emergency that should be (peaceably) answered. Most people, in most of the world, consider it natural and normal to claim dominion over other animals.

And if rescue from the cage, though benign, falls short of a true challenge to the system, then how much more likely is it that insults and threats and violence will fail entirely? The animal-rights position is best suited to foster the idea that violence should be transcended, starting at the roots. In this view, the ethical view, animal-rights activists are also peace activists. And even if they allow pragmatic concerns to guide them, they can hardly afford to be anything but peaceful. The animals we relentlessly subjugate are not in a position to make collective demands, and therefore, to the animal-rights movement, public support is essential.

But the movement promises much back to society. Today, when violations of human rights occur, we hear of people being treated as animals are treated. Were the interests of nonhuman beings taken seriously, expectations about the way humans treat one another would stand to gain. That's not just a selling point to win over human-rights supporters, but an invitation to see our causes as interwoven. A movement which seeks to challenge the distinction between humans and others is necessarily holistic; it sees human life as part of conscious life. Respecting the individual is respectful to the whole. Or, as my friend, the vegetarian restaurant owner, would say, supporting the life force in turn supports everyone in the world.

Some people make commitments that transcend the conventions in which we grew up, but still they confine their iconoclasms within narrow boundaries. Quentin Crisp wrote about people who, notwithstanding their resolve to defy the convention of heterosexuality, quickly adopt new uniforms of dress and speech. What is the purpose of struggling through all those layers of convention, asked Crisp, merely to arrive at another form of convention? The militant advocate revels in convention. Militants recklessly ignore the very foundations of an "animal rights" movement. Nothing could contradict a respectful purpose more starkly than their willingness to present a message through force and fear.

And now we have animal advocates accepting the idea that devotion to the cause means, for an activist identified as young and female, stripping every Friday afternoon at the circus or fur shop. Or bundling up vegetarian treats for the troops, including pin-up style calendars of Kimberley Hefner for soldiers to take along with them as they descend on Iraq.

Some people say war and peace are not matters for animal advocacy. In early 2003, animal-welfare organizer Ingrid Newkirk penned a letter to Palestinian leader Yasser Arafat. The letter took Arafat to task over another Palestinian's use of a donkey in a bomb attack on the West Bank. Newkirk asked Arafat to "appeal to all who listen to you to leave animals out of this conflict." Newkirk showed no corresponding concern over military attacks that kill human beings, and, with the air of someone speaking down from the clouds of Mount Olympus, told the *Washington Post*, "It's not my business to inject myself in human wars."

What, then, is the significance of a campaign such as the one for which Newkirk eventually issued an apology: the *Holocaust on Your Plate*? Is imagery of people wasting away in concentration camps to be used only as a prop? A tendency to attract controversy about human rights issues while taking no moral position on them does not merely distract from the animal advocacy message. It flags a deeper problem. It suggests that advocates fail to grasp what the message of respecting conscious beings is fundamentally about. It is therefore not surprising that Newkirk's campaigns have channelled resources into pressing McDonald's to use gas chambers to kill chickens at the same time they've compared factory farms to Nazi death camps.[6]

Effective animal advocacy has to be about other matters of healing, other matters of justice. This is because the use of animals is fundamentally about domination, and when one goes to the root of the matter, pulling at any aspect of the problem will begin to unearth the whole. One cannot selectively feed the roots of hierarchical thinking; if any domination is reinforced, so is the whole culture that's based on hierarchy and that teaches hierarchy. The more efforts we make to seek a holistic perspective, then, the more likely a movement can emerge to effect deep and lasting change in human psychology. Jeffrey Moussaieff Masson writes both about animal consciousness and the human capacity for gentleness and respect. In a book about the latter, *Lost Prince*, Masson tells the true story of Kaspar Hauser, released at the age of sixteen from a basement cell. One of the more detailed profiles of Hauser was published by Jakob Friedrich Binder, the mayor of Nuremberg, who reported that the teenager, upon being freed from years of near-complete isolation, had no concept of dividing people into sexes. Hauser eschewed meat, would not harm insects, and had sympathy even for the abusive stranger with the key to the basement cell. To Masson, the documentation on Kaspar Hauser suggests that, at least in the case of one human being, the pursuit of bullying, exploiting, controlling, ranking or simply classifying others are occupations that have to be purposefully taught. Ironically, Hauser's imprisonment and subsequent murder were attributed to the suspicion that the child originally held a uniquely high place in German hierarchy, as the heir to the throne of Baden, a Grand Duchy in the German Empire.

As Masson makes clear, the possibility of learning something from Hauser's situation in no way justifies the wrong done to this youth. If the reports about Hauser have a message, though, it is that hierarchical thinking should be challenged wherever it is found, and that such challenges have potential, for hierarchical thinking might not be universally natural. And if hierarchical concepts are taught, they can be changed.

*We must be the change we wish to see, not the
darkness we wish to leave behind.*

MOHANDAS K. GANDHI

The Vandals Took the Handles

I n the spring of 2005, vandals visited a flower nursery in eastern
Pennsylvania. The flower grower, Michael Hsu, had submitted
preliminary paperwork with the intention of building a kennel on
the premises, to store monkeys before they would be shipped to
laboratories.

Monkeys handily win people's sympathy, and local opposition to the
idea of importing, storing, and shipping animals for experimentation was
recorded in the press. Gentle activism in a residential area could have been
enough to build a critical mass of opposition to the application. Word-of-
mouth resistance was moving steadily along that very track, and earned
some thoughtful ink in Allentown's *Morning Call*. But then the whole
story shifted.

Intruders arrived at night, overturned rare Chinese tree peonies, damaged the car of a tenant living on the grounds, and spray-painted obsceni-
ties and the Animal Liberation Front acronym on walls. An anonymous,
e-mailed communiqué warned the property owner to change plans "or we

will destroy your lives." Citing insurmountable difficulties meeting township space requirements, Michael Hsu withdrew the application.

The ransacking of Hsu's greenhouse drew sharp words in the Philadelphia opinion columns. "Animal lovers? No, just bullies," snapped one *Philadelphia Inquirer* columnist. Residents could easily forget, or be forgiven for doubting, that the nighttime visitors came in the name of a gentle ideal. The choice of intimidation as a method suggests that the protesters identified with coercion instead. The fate that the monkeys would have met in transit to laboratories, had Hsu not withdrawn the application and had it been approved, stopped receiving attention. It became impossible to focus solely on the use of the monkeys, or to make larger moral arguments about experimentation without consent. Advocates became obliged to address the tactics of intimidation.

The news that vandals were afoot appeared to gratify only the conservative lobbyists. The U.S. Sportsmen's Alliance had been pressing Pennsylvania's senators to enact House Bill 213, which would strengthen the state's hunter harassment law by making obstruction of hunting an act of eco-terrorism, and significantly increase penalties for property violators whose intent is to "intimidate" or "prevent or obstruct" activities involving animals, plants, or natural resources. How delightful for fans of draconian law to see Michael Hsu telling Pennsylvania senators that the nursery's garden is open to the public, and adding: "We are very concerned about safety now."

Pennsylvania's lawmakers passed the bill in early 2006, and the governor signed it into effect in April.

Each individual state may legislate its own definitions of terrorism and enact relevant laws at any time, and a number of states have accepted eco-terror laws, following prompts by the American Legislative Exchange Council, or ALEC, a collective established by Paul Weyrich of the right-wing Heritage Foundation. ALEC's legislative priorities have helped to ensure a flow of detainees, in turn benefiting the burgeoning private prison industry.[1] This mix is a recipe for applying special scrutiny to people with a particular viewpoint, and for ensuring that classic civil disobedience – picketing a mall that stocks animals, for example, or staging a sit-in at the headquarters of an agricultural business that's polluting waterways – will be stigmatized as terrorism, and punished harshly.

Consider, for example, the Animal and Ecological Terrorism Act championed by the U.S. Sportsmen's Alliance and ALEC. One version of the model, the Oklahoma Farm Animal, Crop, and Research Facilities Protection Act, passed in Oklahoma in 2003; a similar bill was promoted the same year in Texas by Republican lawmaker Ray Allen, who claimed to be "monitoring the growing violence among the growing fringe of animal rights groups and eco-freaks."[2] The Texas bill, as originally introduced, was meant to stop photography intended to "defame" an enterprise, to increase penalties for organizations acting with "an intent to influence a governmental entity or the public to take a specific political action" and to broadly define animal rights or ecological terrorist organizations as "two or more persons organized for the purpose of supporting any politically motivated activity intended to obstruct or deter any person from participating in an activity involving animals or an activity involving natural resources." Had it passed, it would have created Internet sites similar to those which register child molesters by name, address, and photo identification.

The Texas proposal to outlaw environmentalists, and perhaps investigative journalists as well, was not unique. It was matched by similar bills in New York and elsewhere. On New Year's Day, 2004, a new California state law went into effect based on ALEC's "Animal and Ecological Terrorism" model that increased penalties for trespassing on animal farms. Ohio enacted Senate Bill 9 in early 2006, identifying as "corrupt activity" that which is deemed "animal or ecological terrorism." Although serious threats, such as contamination of the food supply, were already covered under criminal law, the new definition does not clearly distinguish between serious threats and expressive advocacy that's been at the core of constitutional political-speech protections.

Wherever such restrictions take hold and harden into law, people are likely to endure lengthy court battles to make law enforcement officers respect their rights to speak and to undertake peaceful collective action. Rather than intimidate communities to the point where repression could actually be welcomed, the key to saving monkeys from being stored in kennels and shuttled to laboratories would be to inspire public sensitivity, and, in turn, a change in the legal climate that takes for granted our instrumental use of other animals.

Not long ago, this approach made considerable inroads when Dan Lyons, through a project named "Uncaged," successfully pressed for an open reading of documents which outlined the state of British organ transplant research. Drug companies had previously obtained an injunction to keep the information confidential. The documents, which chart six years of a race to supply an unlimited supply of animal organs for medical purposes, revealed protocols carried out by the testing firm Huntingdon Life Sciences for a subsidiary of Novartis, in which tissues were transplanted from genetically altered piglets to young monkeys' necks and abdomens. Technical failures had killed numerous primates. A Novartis spokesperson admitted "several significant" mistakes but said the company was committed to ensuring similar mistakes would never be repeated.

But the documents reveal hundreds of errors and omissions, including failure to record organ weights, a quadruple overdose, and conflicting pathology reports. On top of this, the British government had actually approved experiments with the intention of using sick babies as the first trial recipients for nonhuman hearts. As one major London paper announced, the public controversy would now pose "[f]undamental questions over the value of vivisection itself."[3] The activists were getting somewhere.

In a triumph for freedom of information, the ensuing controversy addressed the potential of cross-species transplantation to introduce new infections into the human population. But to the biotech companies, the publicity was troubling. Huge profits were at stake for the first firm to achieve stable transplants from nonhumans into humans. So the pharmaceutical companies covered up their failings – reportedly with help from government officials who reassured pharmaceutical representatives that a key licensing meeting would be a "rubber-stamping" exercise.

Ethics problems are not restricted to any one country. At the moment, a team of U.S. and Korean cloning and stem cell researchers with key roles in the Stem Cell Hub project, which envisioned California and Oxford labs in addition to a laboratory in Korea – scientists who just months earlier were viewed as having science's most promising answers to hospital organ shortages – fell from grace in the midst of a high-profile case of fraud. These scientists too used both human and nonhuman subjects in their experiments.

There is a notion, usually operative but suspended in times of temporary scandal, that researchers, as experts in their field, should be left alone to do what they must for the public good. In reality, history offers many examples of dangerous experiments being performed on vulnerable subjects. Jefferson Davis, lying in a New Orleans charity hospital, accepted a chimpanzee's kidney after doctors told him he would die otherwise.[4] In January 1964, Dr. James Hardy of the University of Mississippi performed the first chimpanzee heart transplant on Boyd Rush, a deaf person with an underprivileged background who entered the hospital unconscious. A stepsister, the only relative who could be located, signed a consent form permitting, if necessary, "the insertion of a suitable heart transplant." Rush lived for two hours after the transplant. In 1984, researchers performed an experimental baboon heart transplant on a dying "Baby Fae" with her mother's questionable consent. Three weeks later, the baby died.

Can we rule out the idea that babies are test instruments and still support science? If so, then an objection to the instrumental use of babies would not be called anti-science. Can we rule out the instrumental use of apes and baboons and still support science? An expansive ethic, one that strives to take seriously a being's own interests, does not doom science; indeed, it respects scientific knowledge about our place within (rather than apart from and above) the animal world.

It makes little sense for bioethicists who claim that making clones out of dogs is necessary for research, for example, to also say that this has nothing to do with the way we as a culture will treat human beings. An ethical borderline between humans and all others has never been found to exist. Information abounds to show that there is no such borderline. Observers in natural and university settings alike have reported that nonhuman primates consciously teach members of their groups distinct cultural traditions. And so, when a panel of twenty-two prominent stem cell researchers, primatologists, lawyers and philosophers debated for more than a year over the ethics of inserting human stem cells into monkey brains, the team's scientists concluded that the science would not let them ethically distinguish humans from other primates. Yet the panel's report, summed up in the July 2005 issue of *Science*, noted (amongst other things) the argument from Genesis that humans are set apart by God.

In Britain's Novartis case, at least fifty baboons were transported from the African savannahs to die in steel cages the size of toilet cubicles. Some, shoved into boxes for transport, died en route to the laboratory. Over a quarter of the primates transplanted with genetically engineered pig hearts and kidneys died as a result of their surgeries, most within hours or days. Researchers described primates dying in fits of vomiting and diarrhoea. Symptoms included violent spasms, bloody discharges, grinding teeth and uncontrollable, manic eye movements. Other animals retreated within themselves, lying still in their cages until put out of their misery. Baboon W205m was "sacrificed" after 21 days. Experimenters noted the pig's heart that had been welded to the arteries in W205's neck had swollen far beyond its natural size, and a yellow fluid was seeping from the organ.

Novartis defended its role at HLS by arguing that developing new cures for humans invariably meant experimenting on live animals.[5] So says God?

Any systematic form of domination and control comes with claims of natural or divine prescription. Acknowledging living individuals' interests in being free from the control of others, people have posited that those interests can be protected through the extension of legal rights. Legal rights, as we've known them, come packaged with an inherent dilemma: The system we call upon to extend them is the very authority that systematically denied them. It's not surprising, then, that the field known as animal law has largely confined itself to asking who gets to speak on behalf of animals rather than ascertaining the animals' real interests.[6]

Although deliberate use of the term "animal rights" is a cue that the advocate seeks to take another's interest seriously, in the animals' reality, the best we can do is appreciate their interest in not needing rights at all – that is, in avoiding the position where they'd need to depend on our protections. Other animals have their own social spheres, and the elaborate details that comprise their life experiences are not understood in terms of access to human civil rights and human institutions. As long as nonhumans are placed inside a game whose rules they don't make, they'll always suffer disadvantages that no ostensible grant of rights can mend. It's simply not plausible that humanity can renounce our privileged position over them, yet live in situations where we *could* exert our will. The very possibility is privilege.

For an illustration of the dilemma, we can turn to Laurence Tribe, a prolific proponent of individual rights. A reporter asked Professor Tribe whether primates could have recourse to courts in their own right. Tribe stated, "Nonhuman animals certainly can be given standing."[7] Yet Tribe has also informed us that "recognizing that a being is entitled to be treated with respect, not wanton cruelty, and an eye to its own flourishing by no means translates into an absolute right, an absolute veto, over any possible use of that entity to save a human life, or achieve a higher goal."

That implies that human needs and goals would trump the needs of unconsenting others. Whether or not that's compatible with biblical texts, it does not fit modern law's professed mission of fundamental fairness. If nonhuman beings really are entitled to the protection of their interests, then experimentation on them is tantamount to torture. No; if animal rights will have any meaning at all, no words get nearer to their core than what Justice Louis Brandeis called "the right to be left alone."[8] The dignity of one's private life, habits, acts, and relations is essential, Brandeis explained, in a way property rights are not, to the "inviolate personality." Justice Brandeis called the right to be left alone the most comprehensive of rights.[9]

Surely, at the core of animal-rights theory is respect for life, freely and fully experienced. Rather than as a resource or part of a number, this theory regards each animal as an inviolate personality with "the right to be left alone." For other animals, the most comprehensive of rights would mean freedom from being the object of popular curiosity; and more: It would mean regaining the freedom from being subjected to our notions of civilization entirely.

Dare we contemplate living independently? Can we? If no other animals inhabited the earth, our remarkably inventive minds could find ethical methods of study. Animal-rights advocates ask that those techniques be found. A widely instructive public presentation on behalf of this view appeared in 2003, after the Uncaged intervention prevailed in the face of injunction requests by the multinational drug producers. While the British government abdicated its responsibility as custodian of the public interests, Uncaged accepted the role, calling for corporate accountability and an open discussion of ethics at a time when the linking of science with bustling commerce has profound and irreversible ramifications. Aghast at the use of pigs, baboons, and, prospectively, human infants, supporters of the Uncaged intervention showed the vital power of informed empathy.

Contrast the press coverage of the Uncaged initiative to the attention that's been attracted to SHAC, which has targeted the same testing firm. SHAC's effort started off with glue in the cash machines of banks servicing Huntingdon, and worked up to brash, personal forms of intimidation. In the autumn of 2004, in the town of Runcorn, England, poison-pen letters appeared at homes and in the public view, singling out people as sex offenders, then urging readers to step right up and confront the accused.

The group's activists in the United States posted the address and phone number of a room in an assisted living residence where stock trader Skip Boruchin's mother lived. The site instructed supporters to "send her sex toys, have an undertaker arrive to pick up her 'dead body,' and call her collect in the middle of the night, pretend to be a friend of Skip's; ask for his cell number in order to place it on the Internet."[10]

Earlier in the year, the media obtained a five-page set of guidelines on harassing executives, workers and families connected, however indirectly, to Huntingdon. One section suggests: "These people need personal loans, salesmen turning up on their doorsteps, funeral services, pornography, pizzas and texts late at night. The possibilities are endless." Alternatively, it suggests widely advertising the target's phone number as a taxi firm to ensure a constant stream of phone calls. The advice continues:

> *If this is all too fluffy for you and you decide to take things a step further, then be very careful. Don't discuss your plans with anyone before or after the action has taken place. If necessary, spend a bit of time putting your target under surveillance.*

The guidelines also recommend burning shoes and clothes worn at the scene, and referring, for further ideas, to the *Bite Back* magazine's online catalogue of attacks, mostly against companies connected to Huntingdon. The list of targets includes 151 names, with explicit contact information. "Whatever you do, just do it and show them no mercy," the document advises.[11] Twenty-one of the targets are children.

Robin Webb, press officer for Britain's ALF, told Scotland's *Sunday Herald* that experimenters' children are "a justifiable target for protest," even while acknowledging that such a view parallels the experimenters' own beliefs in using animals. Webb stated,

> *Some say it is morally unacceptable but it is equally unacceptable to use animals in experiments. The children of those scientists are enjoying a lifestyle built on the blood and abuse of innocent animals. Why should they be allowed to close the door on that and sit down and watch TV and enjoy themselves when animals are suffering and dying because of the actions of the family breadwinner?[12]*

That assumes the only alternatives are either to frighten the children or not frighten them, and that frightening them is the better option. But when faced with actions that seek to threaten rather than persuade, people quite naturally react, rather than respond, to them. Few writers will find it pressing, when contemplating hit lists, to ask fundamental questions about the value of vivisection itself. SHAC campaigns have encouraged the use of scare tactics against virtually any person, no matter how attenuated their link to the targeted testing companies, and in spite of their unexplored potential as allies in the cause of social change. The idea that now children should be intimidated brings this style of activism to a low-water mark – denoting the level at which many news reporters are content to float.

People who wonder if it's possible to model determined activism – without resorting to methods "equally unacceptable" to the ways of thinking that they'd like to change – can take heart from people like Joan Court, a retired nurse who undertook a three-day hunger strike.[13] Court, who once worked with Gandhi, sat at the primate laboratory construction site at Oxford University and slept in a nearby van at night. Interviewed by a newspaper reporter, Court simply explained, "Life is sacred and we should preserve it." Court concluded the strike by eating a dish of vegan stew, thereby publicly connecting the brief strike with the idea of living day-to-day with moral purpose.

Soon afterward, in early 2006, the Animal Liberation Front had vowed to step up their campaign against Oxford University's new £20 million laboratory, calling for protestors to indiscriminately target people with ties to the school – staff, students, teachers, contract workers. University officials, pointing out that charitable bodies with links to the university were being threatened, obtained an unprecedented injunction. Previously restricted to just one protest per week, activists are now restricted to one hour in the afternoon to use megaphones – protesters often use horns, whistles and play tapes of dogs howling – and, after prime minister Tony Blair held a private meeting with university figures, industry leaders and police, the activists have been forbidden to photograph or videotape students, staff, or construction workers. Up to 100 security experts, including former soldiers, have been recruited for the "counter-surveillance" operations at the university, and protection of key workers.

Joan Court had already won wide support in the non-violent resistance against Cambridge University's plans to build Europe's largest primate laboratory, and earned the public approval of Oxford Green Party councillor Matt Sellwood. Frustrated with public confusion after militants focused a threat campaign against Oxford students, Sellwood undertook to show the vital distinction between respect for non-violent resistance and the promotion of authoritarian tactics by briefly marching in an Oxford counter-demonstration – that is, *a protest against the protesters* – under a banner saying "Vegetarians Against the ALF."

...whenever a line is drawn,
it passes through someone's flesh.

RAVEN KALDERA

A Commitment to Respect, and a Handy Pull-Out Guide to Animal Rights

N

o matter how compelling an activist's presentation might be, prevailing attitudes about biomedical research can't be changed in a vacuum. The Uncaged campaign implicitly notes this. It concludes that primate experimentation ought to end, but is less clear on the matter of pigs. A ban on the use of pigs would have to break through the reality that society sees pigs specifically as things to be consumed.

Nextran, a New Jersey- based subsidiary of Baxter International, has bred genetically engineered pigs. The company's activities have resembled the transplantation experiments confronted by the Uncaged initiative. Working with Duke University scientists, Nextran received government clearance to start human trials using the pigs' livers.

Although there is no U.S. version of the Uncaged project, Nextran's vice president of R&D, John Logan, acknowledged that ethical questions arise in the use of both human and nonhuman beings. But while conceding that "[t]he ethical issue surrounding the use of animals is a tough question,"

Logan stated: "With pigs, it's a little clearer. We breed and grow 90 million a year for food...In some sense, society as a whole has made that decision, that the pig can be grown for human uses."[1]

Logan's point is well taken. The acceptance of engineered, cloned, or patented animals exists along a path which began with the agreement that humans can capture, domesticate, commodify, and consume other conscious beings.

Still, some consider the emerging technology beyond the pale. Brazil, India, and Norway, for example, have declined to grant patents to plants and animals. The Uncaged intervention could rightly claim a success to the extent that it has had the audacity to question the white-coated expertise of modern science and industry that intermeddles in nature's evolutionary progress. The value of this instigation can hardly be measured, once it begins to inspire and empower ordinary people.

At the same time, there must be a context: a peaceful educational initiative that works at the bottom line. Any society that deems animals a food item will hardly be prepared to give up biomedical research out of respect for other lives. The likelihood of individuals or cultures asking fundamental ethical questions about vivisection is not strong where those same people routinely interact with other animals by eating them.

Once a person does make a commitment to respect animals in the simplest, most obvious, day-to-day way – by not consuming them – then other, more complex ideas, such as replacements for pesticides and pharmaceutical testing, can begin to fall into place.

Animal Rights: What Is It?

Animal rights is the development of respect for the interests of conscious beings in living on their terms rather than under human dominion.

Animal rights, like ethics, is understood most clearly not as a plural term, but in the singular. Animal rights is not a list of things we give, but an attitude of respect.

The arguments against animal rights are largely irrelevant to its essence. Conscious beings are not attempting to get into our social contracts, enjoy privileges without corresponding responsibilities, or impose complex rules of conduct upon us.

Animal rights, as distinguished from the extension of humane welfare provisions, is fundamentally an issue of justice. The more justice prevails, the less charity is needed. Thus, the guiding principle here isn't to help them, but to aspire not to interfere. At essence, it would mean their privacy from our intrusions.

The advent of animal rights philosophy in a truly radical, egalitarian form would defy millennia of social conditioning. It is, at essence, the repudiation of violence, of seeing others as instruments to our ends, of taking advantage.

The advent of animal rights philosophy would mean the most comprehensive peace movement ever known. Not only would it turn swords into ploughshares; it would dedicate those ploughshares to an agriculture of peace.

Animal rights is the cultivation of ethics without borders.

Chapter Six

This and no other is the root from which a tyrant springs; when he first appears he is a protector.

Plato

The Activist as Superhero

I ntegrity, for the animal rights proponent, rules out scare tactics. Integrity – which we might simply define as integrating the theory of animal rights with one's activism – objects to the music that leads youthful listeners into prison halls, played by pipers who concede that they're unwilling to break the windows themselves, while pointing out which windows need breaking.

There was once a time when people claiming to act on behalf of the Animal Liberation Front professed to take every precaution not to endanger life. Where such a policy is taken seriously, it's a strong statement of principle, and it could also screen people who would sabotage activism. But recent commentary by individual press officers for the group has started to push the envelope – pressing the ALF to accept an overwhelming mass of rhetoric that contradicts that original agreement.

The North American Animal Liberation Press Officers state, with the italics just as they appear here, that the ALF "migrated to the U.S. in the early 1980s and is now an international movement in over twenty countries.

Learning from other liberation movements from around the world, animal liberation activists have now begun to utilize a wider range of tactics shown to be effective, *including the use of force to stop perpetrators of massive violence against non-human animals.*" In a recent article in Scotland's *Sunday Herald*, the British ALF press officer frankly suggested that sympathy for this view is growing:

> *When you look at other struggles, there comes a point where non-violent action no longer works. If activists become fed up with non-violent protest then they will take another road and adopt an armed struggle. When you have right on your side, it's easy to keep going. It really is.*[1]

Those who have right on their side should keep it there. If we say rational debate cannot carry the day, or that the violent acts of exploiters necessitate response in kind, we mock a movement's core principle, we deride its integrity. The show-no-mercy model of militant activism does just that, without any misgivings apparent. It does not pause to reflect on the values underlying the cause it claims to advance. It dismisses consistency; it has no interest in setting forth an integrated purpose or plan. Those who care about the movement's philosophy, its theory or its goals, it treats with suspicion or open disdain.

Some militants appear to view the animals' cause as the latest counter-cultural niche. A new entrant into the militant scene can find a world entirely apart from the banalities of home life: metal bands, tattoos and body piercings, being locked together inside of Neiman Marcus to protest fur, occupying professors' offices, seeing one's name in the papers, hosting speakers, and being initiated into an activists' circle by going on night surveillance trips and undercover investigations. More than just a fashion, militant activism beckons the one who's searching for an identity, and offers a ready-made enemy and a ready-made group of friends – who, like the animals, become victims to avenge. SHAC's Kevin Kjonaas urges support for the Animal Liberation Front because the U.S. system "unconstitutionally disadvantages those noble few who break unjust laws to help animals," and although ALF activists are "selfless in their actions and are not asking for help," activists "owe them our support...by means of exploiting the press attention they stir, by writing our letters of support to those who are captured, and by discussing their contributions within a proper historical context."[2]

A quick rise to leadership (and press attention) is possible, for militant animal advocacy is a small pond. In a community that's thought to have a high female presence, showy male leadership is common. Indeed, if one consciously hoped to preserve an atmosphere that promotes male leadership, one might put a special premium on physical force and destructive displays. Consciously or not, that choice is made.

The Earth Liberation Front emerged in 1992 when activists felt that Earth First! tactics were too timid. Earth First! itself was formed in 1980 by Dave Foreman and several other activists who thought the environmental groups in the late 70s were too staid. "We prided ourselves on being buckaroos," remembers Tim Mahoney about working with Foreman. "We could outstomp and outdrink the others. We wanted to show that to be for wilderness you didn't have to be an effete Brie-eater. ...We weren't going to concede who were the cowboys." In Foreman's own words, "We let off a lot of steam for the first couple of years."[3]

Still associated with the steam is Paul Watson, who calls himself "the first man to put his body between a harpoon and a whale."[4] Watson co-founded Greenpeace in the 1970s but left to establish the more confrontational Sea Shepherd Conservation Society, whose ships physically obstruct crews it finds making illegal catches. One writer describes the activist group's boat as carrying "a huge water gun; it would be used to splurt whalers and drift netters with 50-gallon globs of cream pie."[5] About such forays, Watson has written:

> *We have the swash buckling reckless courage to take a stand against these destroyers because on the high seas, it is these poachers, these long-liners, these whalers, these sealers, these draggers, drift-netters, seiners, and*

polluters who are the pirates of greed and we – the pirates of kindness and salvation.[6]

It is this good-against-evil template that environmental and animal advocacy militants apply to a variety of circumstances. The "other side" has a cruel glint in its collective eye; it's presumably impervious to either kindness or wisdom and it must be found and attacked. A scan of the press reports, graffiti, and e-mail alerts shows authoritarian activism typically setting out to make two main points:

1. *Plunder of the earth or cruelty to animals goes on with impunity; and*
2. *Now the scum will pay.*

The followers of this strain accept that might is right and when push comes to shove, in the words of SHAC activist Kevin Kjonaas, the activist must be "ready to push, kick, shove, bite, do whatever to win."[7] Kjonaas explains, "I spent a year in England working full time on animal rights campaigns and there really cut my teeth on some 'true grit' activism."[8]

Mark Potok spoke about this attitude at Friends of Animals' conference held in Manhattan in July 2005. The event, named "Foundations of a Movement," focused on the relationship between animal advocacy and the greater movement to eradicate prejudice; and Potok, who, along with colleagues at the Southern Poverty Law Center, has paid increasingly keen attention to "the greening of hate," described trends in environmental and animal advocacy that parallel the growth of right-wing extremism. Potok has researched violent ideology for two decades, and did not water down the message. Taking responsibility for activism, rather than letting it fall into violence-prone hands, could head off a revenge killing in the name of animal rights, and the media mess and the complete ruin that would surely follow. Such a calamity does not materialize out of thin air, explained Potok; an avenger mentality seeks certain group characteristics, tending to include arrogance or closed-mindedness; a preference for ready-made classifications and assumptions about groups of people over sociological knowledge; and a propensity to find evil-doers. Hostile attitudes displayed both by right-wing extremists and animal-welfare or environmental militants might be reflected in tattoos depicting fires or similar symbols of identification with the cause. Both ideologies identify enemies that endanger or oppress the members' allies and dependents, who must, in turn, be protected or avenged.

Seriously considering this warning took effort, both on the part of the conference planners and those who came to participate. But the activists who organized the event decided that it would be would be brash and unwise to dismiss, without examination, critical advice from a sincere observer. And that to dismiss it from one who studies and engages in social activism would be outright negligence. And perhaps that the acceptance of some significant part of the critique, meaning that a certain project would have to be re-thought, would not make any activist a failure. That a change in perspective, when we accept that such change is warranted, signals personal growth, and that would make sense if we we're to see a nuanced movement take shape.

Probably the best known act of ideologically based destruction in recent times, the 1998 burning of a lodge on Vail Mountain to protest ski resort expansion, frightened activists away from the environmentalist cause in the midst of an investigation of the $12 million in damage.[9] A key question arises here: Why would activist groups overlook setbacks brought about by destructions, or notice them, but continue on in the same way? After all, when the actions of a demonstrator divert public attention from the movement's message, or turn a corporate plunderer into a public victim, or otherwise resemble acts conceived by someone attempting to discredit the movement, then that demonstrator's tactic is probably a bad one.

Some activists surely notice the problem. Their complaint – a rather self-fulfilling one – is that they just aren't getting anywhere with diligence alone, and that change shouldn't wait. Then there is the ritual, the need to mark up wins. This impatience has a particular appeal to young people.

Militant activists who decide on advocacy as a long-term career path typically move into professionalized welfare advocacy. The pressure to score victories often intensifies here, as the advocacy group expects the activist to garner publicity, attract members, and keep the donor base satisfied. And so it is that rescue announcements and victory messages and marches, the award ceremonies, the speaking invitations, and the celebrity advertisements unfurl in a constant panorama of individual achievements and personalities.

This synthesis of frustration and a longing for personal success can explain the urge to seek and magnify small, meaningless, or even backward steps. Hens have been freed from their cages, and dear public, please don't ask whether they're still crammed into sheds, just eat, drink, and be merry – and don't forget to donate. Mother pigs will be taken out of crates, great victory!; dear public, don't ask whether the industry had already resolved to do without the crates because they impede piglet survival rates, cutting into profit. Chickens will no longer be electrocuted; soon we'll gas them to death; there'll be a party on Friday. Lab chimpanzees are *retired*, kept fed by your generous donations, dear public; don't ask whether the titles are still held by the government, thereby making *warehoused* the more accurate term.

And each distortion of animal-rights theory for the gratification of a quick victory announcement, every politically expedient compromise that stops some use of animals only to stimulate another form of it, each assertion that the institutions which commodify animals can bring us closer to respecting those animals – every one represents a lost opportunity to publicly demonstrate the value of taking animal rights seriously.

If the craving for little victories seems more pronounced in animal advocacy than in other areas of progressive activism, it's partly because the nonhuman beneficiaries can't hold activists accountable for stopping short of serious change. And this suits a money-driven society well. People in general don't want to take activists seriously. They don't like change that strikes them as too radical, too personal, too likely to erode property or transform livelihoods as we know them today into something yet unknown.

Agreements with corporations, in contrast, offer predictable rewards. They can effectively promote both the industries that use animals and those that advocate for welfare improvements. Hence, many an animal advocacy group spends the better part of its time focused on dreary details about the use of antibiotics, the numbers of animals in a cage, the dimensions of a shed, an animal's age at the time of slaughter, or whether an animal is properly stunned before dying. A peculiar aspect of the bulk of today's animal advocacy – including militant activism – is that it's primarily concerned about how to treat animals once they're already under our collective thumb.

Groups objecting to the practice of dragging sick and immobile cattle point out that it's impossible to transport disabled cows humanely. As though, with the right advice, humane transport would be the norm for animals moving through the $38 billion dollar cattle flesh industry.[10] Humane-treatment advocates have also seized on the discovery of mad cow disease in the state of Washington, and stated that a change in practice would restore consumer confidence in the U.S. beef industry – sounding much like experts for the industry itself. Although cattle transport reforms had nothing to do with the interests of cows, but were advanced simply so the sale of cattle for human consumption could continue, professional advocates portrayed the government's moves as a victory and did not hesitate to associate them with their own campaigning. They had established their value as consultants to agribusiness.

Bird flu has loomed on the global radar screen since January 2004, when the World Health Organization released a detailed alert on avian influenza and the significance of its transmission to humans. For some people, it was the first time they heard about birds splattered in excrement or the pervasive use of antibiotics and the battered immune systems of birds in the stream of commerce. Healthful eggs, we shouldn't wonder, have been in increasingly high demand.

Whether the disease would be best contained through big industry's biosafety measures or through improved husbandry became a point of contention. Less intensive chicken farming was the preferred idea of Dr. Perry Kendall, the chief medical officer for British Columbia, Canada, who said that birds packed 10,000 to a shed are "more frail and more vulnerable to diseases" and can act like a petri dish when "there are so many of them in such a small volume of space."[11] No matter who was correct, the obvious best answer is to stop eating birds, but humane advocacy groups put the bulk of their money on cage-free farming – liberally citing Dr. Kendall.

More careful husbandry in the bird factories would be expensive, but the potential of folding human health concerns into general animal-welfare advertising was not lost on upmarket companies. From the spring of 2004, the Trader Joe's chain announced plans to "improve its laying hen welfare policy" by marketing house brand eggs that aren't from "cruel cages." As advocates issued the victory announcements, the grocery's CEO, Dan Bane, trumpeted the good business move. "Customers looking for cage-free eggs will need to look no further than the Trader Joe's label," said Bane, indicating an expectation that the fancy house brand will enjoy a marketing edge over the other eggs sold by the chain. "We expect this change will help further boost the proportion of sales of cage-free eggs at Trader Joe's."[12]

The government sets no rules for "cage-free" production, and finding that term on a box of eggs does not mean the company met any particular standard. But even if corporations were to take free-range seriously – not just removing cages, but buying access to fresh air and pasture – they'd necessarily be marketing to consumers who can pay for the bodies of animals who, when living, took up the most space. This is obviously bizarre. Already, most of the landmass of the contiguous United States is taken up by agriculture – primarily for resource-guzzling animal processing. Meanwhile, as precious time passes, other life is pushed to the margins of the land. Brushed aside are the animals living on nature's terms, those who might have a chance to keep their territory and thus their freedom, those whose appearance would evoke not pity but exhilaration. As activists celebrate and plan awards over the removal of crates at some industrial farm, free animals are slowly dying out of range, farther off into the rocks, the deserts, the tundra. Everywhere it spreads, animal agribusiness begets deforestation, creates monocultures, and relies on massive doses of chemical pesticides. From both an animal-rights and an environmental perspective, it makes no sense to ask for bigger ranges for animals no one should eat.

And still, most advocates, militants included, are squarely involved in conceptualizing relief from the worst scenarios. The Animal Liberation Front's first guideline now states that a member is expected "[t]o liberate animals from places of abuse, i.e. laboratories, factory farms, fur farms, etc., and place them in good homes where they may live out their natural lives, free from suffering."[13] No simple statement about animal agribusiness appears; we instead find factory farms distinguished as suitable targets.

Note the values enshrined in the prescription. The ALF member is to focus on animals in situations where they are systematically made useful to, and in virtually every case fully dependent upon, human owners. The use isn't questioned; rather, *abuse* is the highlighted term. No mention of animals' natural interests in experiencing the risks and benefits of living on their own terms; rather, the ALF is concerned with the *avoidance of suffering*.

No animals inhabiting the earth in freedom would benefit from our attempting to make their lives free from suffering, for the capacity to experience pain enables an animal to seek and find safety. If respect means we avoid instigating others animals' suffering, to be consistent we'd reject the idea that we could extinguish it, as that would be just as intrusive, and grossly unnatural. But it isn't freedom that rivets the modern ALF guidelines.[14] Instead, the mission focuses on conditions within the institutions that use animals. Multiple contradictions inhabit the concept that "natural" lives can be lived out in "good homes" and that the orchestration of such arrangements constitutes "liberation." Husbandry – that is, attention to conditions of the captive animals – is an element of the socially acceptable control people wield over animals pursuant to laws and administrative regulations. In the case of the ALF, we have one more layer to ensure animal welfare: the vigilante enforcement of husbandry principles. The militant, according to the ALF's paradigmatic guidelines, still wields control over other animals, acting within a traditional welfare role.

Militant campaigns frequently target companies that defy the husbandry standards governing laboratories – called, depending on the country one lives in, animal-welfare standards or good laboratory practices. Videos and posters against Huntingdon depicted wounded dogs, and puppies being punched or suffering other grotesque and wanton cruelties. ("Someone punched a dog in our lab," a Huntingdon spokesperson admitted, "and it was terrible, but it was an isolated incident."[15]) The campaign to stop Huntingdon was not animated by a proposal to question humanity's domination of dogs or mice or guinea pigs in the first place. A strategy to draw public sympathy? Undoubtedly, horror and pity were seen as indispensable to the mission. Perhaps some of the campaigners accepted the underlying premise that the animals can be used, if used as gently as institutional resources will permit. In any case, the public did not hear the message that animals should not be under our thumb. The violent videos and the bloody posters were far too prominent for that discussion to emerge. The complaint was not that the animals were being used by Huntingdon, but rather that they were being *abused* by Huntingdon.

For proof of their point, activists turned to institutional authority, citing the administrative fines the company had incurred. In other words, multiple aspects of the SHAC campaign appear to form an argument for good laboratory practices. And the company has responded with public assurances that the animals, mostly rodents, end up being killed in the most humane way possible. It's easy to miss the fundamental question about use and believe this is largely a debate over who will enforce rules against abuse. Recently, a testing lab owned by a company named Covance was infiltrated by an undercover agent who taped various activities. The infiltrator told the media that the observations would have stopped straight away if the lab were operating according to the rules. That is, the agent would have walked out and no one would have known anyone was spying at all.

Working on eliminating the worst harms of certain corporations or industries becomes a matter of subjective decision-making, and it also perpetually chases the outer edges of commercial uses. Companies grow, new uses are thought up. The inherent growth needs of a profit-based society advance animal use in new ways each year. Activism simply can't compete by chasing after these institutions' worst abuses.

The prison system keeps growing as well, and one of its raw materials is the militant. Champions of intimidation are handing critiques, ready-made and gift-wrapped, to the public and to the authorities. Threats and fires serve as grim public examples of what happens when caring for animal suffering goes too far. In the eyes of the militants, though, the Animal Liberation guidelines offer opportunities for independent action. Militants cite negative media attention as proof that the system has really been challenged. But a contrary force is often at work. Do something that makes the movement look unethical and counterproductive, or even silly, and yes, the news companies might well notice.

"We ask nicely for years and get nothing," say the champions of intimidation. "Someone makes a threat, and it works."[16] Of course it does not work, if the goal is to achieve respect for other living individuals. It does not work, if the goal is to begin establishing a movement. The point of a social movement is not to oppose people with whom its members disagree. The point of a movement is to cultivate an alternative viewpoint, one that takes hold, gains energy, and becomes plausible to enough people to effect a paradigm shift. In contrast, the goal of the threat is immediate attention, usually negative. I am reviled; therefore I am. This means falling into the pattern of acting as a negative, existing in response to what one opposes – in effect, reinforcing the opposed position as the standard.

Catharine MacKinnon observes, "People tend to remain fixated on what we want from them, to project humans onto animals, to look for and find or not find ourselves in them."[17] What do advocates want from animals? Sites and brochures showing scenes of cruelty and rescue do not paint a picture of an animal's natural power, autonomy, or grace. They confirm an animal's victimhood, and the rescuer's correlative strength. This imagery is equally fostered in brash militancy and public charity. Both the animal-welfare militants and the big animal-protection groups aspire to wield control and influence policy, and both forms of advocacy rely strongly on the caretaking model. Sanctuaries know that rescues bring in waves of donations; public attention can be sustained by "adoptions" of needy animals, and sanctuary supporters' sites commonly offer infantilized descriptions of the animals in their care. Some rescue sites go so far as to dress the animals up for newsletters, adult animals become Special Little Ones, and picture galleries are peppered liberally with diminutive terms usually reserved for small children. In same cases, the strength of the animal-welfare activist over the animal is taken to its most stark conclusion, as the rescuer kills. People for the Ethical Treatment of Animals uses a barbiturate, sodium pentobarbital, to kill by one injection into the dog's or cat's leg. "The animal is held lovingly and petted and talked to as the solution enters the vein," the group's president explains. "For many of these animals, that is the only loving touch they have ever felt."[18]

Feminists have observed the ways in which society's extension of protection to women as a bargain that ends up with the women still under control. That is, women often end up appealing to protective men to guard them from harmful men, reinforcing the systematic reliance on male control rather than eroding it. As capability to do violence becomes equated with nobility, vulnerability and dependence become romanticized. The more firmly a social group can demand respect, the less it requires forms of protection, and the less it allows paternalistic notions of welfare to hungrily feed on theories of just violence.

In the same style as the male protector, the animal advocate might vaunt a powerful persona; as we've seen, advocates might view themselves as entitled to make life-or-death decisions for animals, either legally, at shelters and refuges, or outside of the law, in raids; or the activities might contain a mix of legal permissions and lawless manoeuvring. At its most vainglorious, the rescuer's identity relies on the idea of a stream of little animals hurt by a stream of inhumane and burly barbarians, and the latter they must bravely engage in combat, like Dudley Do-Right riding up to save the day after a black-caped Snidely Whiplash has tied Nell to the railroad tracks.

The appeal of this simplistic plot – enemy attacks victim; rescuer comes to save the victim and vanquish the evil-doer – encourages the self-certitude seen in a wide range of political activism. It's the human propensity to identify one group as the enemy that is perpetrating some evil upon another group, allowing the latter to define one's purpose. The narrative accommodates an enemy, a rescuer, and the victim, and the experiences of the victim matter just as far as they further the narrative. The victim is an object. By identifying the victimized other as a sacred emblem of the cause, one can reduce any activist purpose to indulgence in authoritarian tactics and in violence. Dressing them up smartly in the language of political activism, the rescuer presents the indulgences as heroic self-sacrifice.

Rather than constantly focusing on this narrative, working for change means breaking the fixation on suffering, and examining the reasons we put forth when we claim dominion over others. The essential question is not who the victims are, or which victims merit the most attention. The essential question is about us – those in the class that, at any given time, decides, argues, declares, and objectifies. What creates our interest in domination? Finding out, and changing our minds, will take time, and strength, and a resolve to deal with everyday difficulties and dialogues that often seem thoroughly unnewsworthy but are understood as real and lasting investments in a movement. That's a far cry from doing what we will in the name of the animals, no matter what people think. Concern for what people think, given that animals can't free themselves, is essential.

CHAPTER SEVEN

Come my friends,
'tis not too late to seek a newer world.

ALFRED, LORD TENNYSON

The War on Terror

The State Department defines terrorism with a focus on violence against people, but the FBI definition of domestic terrorism encompasses any politically motivated crime. Even a protest of graffiti on a billboard could be arguably construed as terrorism under the definition, derived from the U.S. Code of Federal Regulations, which counts "the unlawful use of force and violence against persons or property to intimidate or coerce the government, the civilian population, or any segment thereof, in furtherance of political or social objectives."[1] The FBI further describes a terrorist incident as "a violent act or an act dangerous to human life, in violation of the criminal laws of the U.S., or of any state, to intimidate or coerce a government, the civilian population, or any segment thereof, in furtherance of political or social objectives." Thus it's whether the act has a social or political purpose, rather than whether or how much it constitutes a threat to others, that brings the stigma of a terrorism charge.

Notably, the U.S. Code also acknowledges that there is no single, universally accepted, definition of terrorism. The FBI has decided to characterize the Animal Liberation Front and the Earth Liberation Front as engaged in eco-terrorism not only when they act, but even when they threaten. Eco-terrorism, according to the FBI, is "the use or threatened use of violence of a criminal nature against innocent victims or property by an environmentally-oriented, subnational group for environmental-political reasons, or aimed at an audience beyond the target, often of a symbolic nature."[2]

Many a writer has discussed terrorism, and the more one sifts through, the more contradictory and complex the answers become. Brent Smith, author of *Terrorism in America*, has noted that "scholars have defined, refined, and redefined terrorism to accommodate personal preferences regarding what should or should not be labeled terroristic."[3] Thus, to a substantial extent, we can assume that the definition of terror will depend on the vested interests of those in the position to influence the defining. Smith adds: "While many criminologists accept the government's legal definitions of crimes (as well as the statistics generated by such definitions), others contend that the study of crime must include, for example, violations of human rights, racism, and other behaviors not explicitly defined as criminal in the legal codes."

Militants and their supporters are likely to nod here, as they point out that "real terror" involves such things as deforestation, global warming and the related spread of disease, toxic wastes and chemical poisoning, cloning and the invention of grotesque hybrids in labs, and accelerated species loss all over the planet. All of these are matters of intense public concern. Also of concern is whether the public will seek the valuable knowledge of dedicated animal-rights or environmental campaigners whose movements become hopelessly connected in the public view with sensational headlines, and with intimidating language and actions.

As coercive activism brings ever more drastic responses from the makers and enforcers of law, the educational efforts of the peaceful majority of activists are subjected to a chilling effect. A website might inform its visitors about the ethical and health issues related to experiments on animals and simultaneously enable the site's visitors to send an "e-protest" to a research council or lawmakers or a cosmetics company. The value of the rights to communicate and to receive such speech is central to our traditional freedom of discussion. One can easily imagine a guest writer visiting an open Internet forum after a rough day and a few beers and expressing the opinion that it would be nice if someone could break a wolf hunter's trap. That the guest has an environmental orientation shouldn't jeopardize an advocacy group's ability to offer the forum, let alone bring the group to the attention of a Joint Terrorism Task Force.

In the 1960s, the U.S. Supreme Court insisted that – even accepting the government has a compelling interest in countering violent revolution – guilt by association "has no place here."[4] Thus emerged the principle of individual culpability: the government may not punish an individual for associating with a group that engages in legal activities unless it proves the person's specific intent to further an illegal action of that group. Both federal and state governments, with their recent willingness to define ecological terrorism as broadly as they can, appear eerily willing to paint dissenters with the broadest legal brush. Good activism should – without needlessly exacerbating the problem by using threats and predictably drawing reactions that will affect an entire viewpoint-based community – point out and steadfastly oppose threats and intimidation to the Constitution.

The *Austin Review*, a conservative journal, printed a comment in April 2003 under the title "Enviro-Terror in Disguise." After enjoying the convenience of being able to quote an employee of an advocates' group who told a conference audience that "blowing stuff up and smashing windows" is a "great way to bring about animal liberation," the commentator set out to dissuade people from giving even to "docile" nonprofits because one might "assume" that "at least some of the members" of one group might have attended events run by another. It's not thought absurd these days for such logic to find public backing. And yet, if someone who said bombing abortion clinics was a great way to achieve a goal, it's most unlikely that the public would see it as a warning about docile Christian groups.

One reason we could expect a different response in the two scenarios is that Christian groups are familiar to most people in this society. Animal advocacy is far less familiar to the public. We could complain that the disparity between the reactions are unfair; alternatively, we could think about how to make animal advocacy familiar to the public. And if the advocacy is consistent, it will model an awareness that violence against animals will not cease as long as people encourage acts of intimidation and violence against other humans. We would denounce bullying conduct – by the government, by a corporation, or by an activist. Because we envision a society capable of transcending the paradigm in which controlling groups terrorize vulnerable groups, we know that meaningful change must come through peaceful action.

So yes, SHAC supporters have a point when they maintain that animal advocacy is seen as a fringe issue, and the government is banking on the broader social justice movement to be less than supportive, and that SHAC's case is "intended to pave the way for further silencing of activists involved in all issues."[5] SHAC's conclusion – that "the broader social justice movement" must "stand behind these activists in our communal defense of free speech, press, and association" – skips over the question of whether animal advocates ought to pave the way for further silencing of activists in various causes, and to make educating the public about their issues more difficult.

There's enormous value in the presence of civil rights lawyers who take the cases of activists. Yet I would suggest that lawyers who are also animal rights theorists have a special responsibility: to inform potential activists that the theory for which they claim to act, seen in its best light, means eschewing violence and working instead to infuse social attitudes with sensible ideas. Minds don't change for the good by force, or by threats, or by seething resentment, and the law becomes an uglier thing when baited by this futile self-expression.

INTERMISSION

Poet and rock musician Patti Smith is on stage in a
New York concert, talking of the wasting of nature.
Man thinks he has conquered the world, Mother
Earth is wringing in wonder, man thinks he has
conquered his Mother, taken everything, every
fossil, every force. But Mother Earth will last.
And eventually Mother Earth is going to rise up.
And shake him off.

And the audience applauds, thinking, that's right,
if man won't wake up from the stupid sleep of
possessing, thinking everything and everyone is a
resource, racing the planet around as though it
were some rented car, then one day when he thinks
he's got it all controlled, she is going to shake him.
That's only natural. Right on.

One problem, thinks the audience.
How did we get stuck with the man?

PART TWO

SEEKING A
NEWER WORLD

Chapter Eight

No morality can be founded on authority,
even if the authority were divine.

A.J. Ayer

The Stewards

Through the centuries, humanity has ranked itself and other beings within hierarchies. We're beginning to question the habit – some now speak of an interconnected web of life – but it's dying hard, if it's dying at all. The conquest of nature has been seen as mandated and promised in authoritative texts, be they religious, philosophical, or scientific. Progress we've called it, that seemingly endless quest human minds have undertaken to transform life into an orderly, risk-free experience by constantly inventing and imposing controls over external factors. It assumes that we're better off forcing the surrounding world to adjust to us than adjusting our mental energies to those of the surrounding world.

Promoting the physical integrity of the human community was once as simple as resolving that it would be acceptable to kill another animal for food, or safety, or the safety of our food. We can only speculate as to how simple that really was. Perhaps it was morally troubling, and inferiority had to be invented, so that we could live with taking the life of another being who clearly shared our own drive to live. Perhaps we had to construct an idea that those who set out to take that life away were not only effective members of the community, but noble too.

Some anthropologists argue that human evolution was shaped, to a large extent, by others: the carnivores. Even today, about 174 kinds of animals prey on primates in various regions of the world, with even the nonhuman great apes vulnerable to leopards and lions. The leopard-bitten skulls of early humans at sites in Asia and Africa, say anthropologists Donna Hart and Robert Sussman, support a "Man, the Hunted" theory of evolution. Without teeth designed for tearing prey, modern humanity's ancestors focused on co-ordinating large groups for protection. As other prey animals do, these communities likely used their excess members – those not necessary to feed infants, for example – as sentinels. All in all, conclude Hart and Sussman, our ancestors probably spent a lot of time dodging predators.

Later in the archaeological record, weapon-making and cooking turn up. Eventually, the custom of vanquishing the other, whether justified by authority brashly presumed or painfully contrived, became a social system of dominating, and then commodifying, other animals. And, like any centuries-old habit lying about in our psyches, this one is hard to break – as a look at the top-selling videos or television shows makes clear. Some future discoverer of the ancient culture called humanity might fairly decide that we *Homo sapiens* were an insecure lot. Until the end, we kept on fighting and vanquishing animals by deliberately ignoring the unremitting destruction of their territory. By ignoring their numbers when they fell in the wars we waged. By the deforestation of their habitat and the expansion of the farming we prized. By only permitting them to exist insofar as we could take advantage of them as tourist attractions, experimental subjects, film props, guards, playthings, or something to package in bright yellow foam and unwrap, ingest, and excrete.

When something or someone prompts people to think about the captive lives that so many of our institutions take for granted, they are likely to rebuff the prompt. "Don't tell me," a friend or parent might say. "I don't want to hear about that." This reaction hardly seems born of indifference. Rather, it arises to deflect moral unease. It's normal to avoid what's disturbing to our sensibilities by simply declining to hear of it. And that's exactly what most people do, for most of our lives.

But a smaller group of people are intrigued by both the moral and social issues involved. People within this group might have careers in breeding, in animal vending, or in panning animal advocates' campaigns. Some know more animal-rights theory than many activists who claim to act in the theory's name. They are particularly interested in what they consider "real" animal-rights advocacy – ideas that go beyond the glaringly obvious abuses to tackle the everyday uses. They join discussion lists; they are devoted to debate, and may engage in it daily. Still, they rebuff the concept of broadening their moral community in a way that would take nonhuman interests seriously. Some repeatedly warn that animal advocacy will lead to the decline of all types of ownership and use of other animals – even though they rarely meet advocates with that unwavering view. Catharine MacKinnon rightly points out that most advocates don't have that view; again, most advocates "tend to remain fixated on what we want from them, to project humans onto animals, to look for and find or not find ourselves in them."

Which, if this hypothesis has any merit, leads us to the most intensely charged scene of the modern human self-preservation drama. Enter the advocates. Here are the people into whose minds the concept of respecting living, conscious individuals really might seep. Is it here that the reaction of humanity makes its most striking appearance? Is it evitable that animal advocates will work against the best interests of their cause? To the extent that an idea appears to threaten self-preservation, such an idea will, understandably, create ambivalence in the person who holds it. If our collective memory warns that animals might eat us unless we assert ourselves as the pre-eminent consumers, and if we decide to challenge that hegemonic human identity, it's understandable that we run into a conflict of interest. There is doubtless a kernel of real anxiety expressed in the quip, "I didn't fight my way to the top of the food chain to be a vegetarian."

Our concept of ourselves as the pinnacle of life is not alien to the modern era of scientific thought, or to spokespeople most frequently invoked by animal advocates. Note, for example, the mission undertaken by Jane Goodall, presented in the book *In the Shadow of Man:*

> *It has come to me, quite recently, that it is only through a real understanding of the ways in which chimpanzees and men show similarities in behavior that we can reflect with meaning on the ways in which men and chimpanzees* differ. *And only then can we really begin to appreciate, in a biological and spiritual manner, the full extent of man's uniqueness.*[1]

The underlying hierarchy was established, although it usually goes unmentioned. But it's visible. The shadow to which Goodall's title refers represents a hierarchy, a ladder of being. "Just as he is overshadowed by us," Goodall proclaims, "so the chimpanzee overshadows all other animals." They are less only because we are more; because they provide useful educational models for us, we're entitled to use them. After differentiating ourselves from them, we call ourselves superior. There's always a difference to be found.

Goodall writes, "It should not be surprising that a chimpanzee can recognize himself in a mirror. But what if a chimpanzee wept tears when he heard Bach thundering from a cathedral organ?" For more than thirty-five years since Goodall asked that question, animal researchers and lawyers alike have insisted that animals jump through higher and higher cognitive hoops to be considered full persons. I believed them myself, some years ago. What has come to me quite recently, thanks in large part to the people acknowledged at the start of this book, is that most of animal advocacy has focused on measuring other animals' similarity to us. Advocacy hasn't comprehended the idea that our measurements might be beside the point. It has also focused largely on the interests of domesticated or captive animals, indicating that most advocates will accept domestication or captivity as long as the animals therein are not flagrantly maltreated.[2]

This is hardly a cause for surprise. Human society itself, structured according to the concept of male dominance, ensures that no one of us has ever enjoyed the personal experience of freedom from hierarchies. We have never known a humanity that applies an egalitarian philosophy to itself. If activists sometimes fail to perceive the inequities, it's because the inequality within humanity is also rendered invisible, or recast as a natural difference.[3] As long as humans do not work to remove the domination pattern from our social relationships, our paradigms of social control continually leach into the relations between humans and the other animals of the planet.

Given all the overt and subtle rules, borders, and restrictions that our elders have taught us to accept and to pass on in turn, how can activists equip ourselves for the enormous moral evolution that taking animal interests seriously would involve? There is simply no handbook. So when people decide to be advocates, they seek roles as rescuers or pet fanciers; as cognitive ethologists or veterinary malpractice specialists. They become zookeepers or zoo advocates. They advocate for free-range meat or cage-free eggs. They seek positions on review boards that approve experimental protocols. They enter the laboratories and work as assistants, or they infiltrate the laboratories and do the same thing. They focus on institutions, isolated from ideas about broader social progress. Thus, many support campaigns that revile workers, or laud tree-spiking or arson or other fear-inducing techniques. Some praise militant anti-abortionists for their consistent beliefs and actions. Some talk a great deal about sending abusers to jail.

Their works are not subjected to any kind of meaningful review to ensure consistency or integrity. But rather than consider how their jumble of incoherent concepts and campaigns must appear to the outer world, activists treat inconsistency as a virtue. Pointing to something one likes in the muddle, the activist declares, "You see? They do some good things." Gripping this dysfunctional compass they cry for unity, or repeat platitudes about the need to "use every tool in our toolbox" or "let a million flowers bloom." All manner of conduct is justified "for the animals" and anyone who points out contradictions is dismissed as lacking in social graces, characterized as divisive, or called a threat to the animals. Steve Best has gone so far as to call principled non-violence a "pro-violence stance" because it fails to take "adequate measures" to stop harm to animals. Best's writings even attempt to enlist Martin Luther King on the side of violence by claiming that King said, "I am only effective as long as there is a shadow on white America of the black man standing behind me with a Molotov cocktail."[4] In a 1968 speech, Dr. King said, "We don't have to argue with anybody. We don't have to curse and go around acting bad with our words. We don't need any bricks and bottles, we don't need any Molotov cocktails."[5] King then encouraged activists the go to the stores, and to the massive industries, ask for fair and right treatment, and, if not heeded, withdraw economic support from them.

That is the advice Professor Best ignores, the advice Best's followers don't hear. By carrying out violence in the name of the animals, these followers, mostly young and untutored in political history, can instantly prove their willingness to sacrifice comfort and freedom, to pay their dues in order to release animal victims from the evil-doers. The activists forget that these evil oppressors also think they are vanquishing evils: world hunger, disease, cancer, the ravages of age. And so, at the Militants' Ball, they dance with their opponents in an endless pas de deux.

"I think for 5 lives, 10 lives, 15 human lives, we could save a million, 2 million, 10 million non-human lives." Thus spoke Jerry Vlasak, a California-based doctor, talking to a conference audience about how the assassination of experimenters could save animals.

Congress was nonplussed. When asked by the Senate committee on environment and public works about the seriousness of that idea, Vlasak affirmed that deadly force "would be a morally justifiable solution" against scientists who use nonhuman animals.[6] New Jersey Senator Frank Lautenberg called Vlasak outrageous, anti-social, and smug before exclaiming, "You're willing to take lives…You're willing to say somebody that you don't know, somebody's kid, somebody's parent, somebody's brother, somebody's sister – take that life, that's okay. Teach those S.O.B.s a lesson."

To which Vlasak replied: "These are not innocent lives."

In the spring of 2005, Vlasak spoke approvingly to Canadian reporters about the use of violence to bring Newfoundland's seal trade to an end, reportedly comparing himself with "lots of people who have taken up arms, like Nelson Mandela and lots of other brave people, who have been to prison and won the Nobel Peace Prize."[7] Vlasak vilified Newfoundland's coast-dwellers who, pursuant to government-issued quotas, kill seals.[8] The kind of holistic intervention that Judi Bari talked about would look quite different. It would view working people as potential allies, so in this case it would exert its economic pressure not on the people who live as near to the poverty line as to the sea, but on the government that fails to engage the human potential of its coastal populace. Vlasak will have none of that. Calling the seal killers "abhorrent," the doctor adds, "The threat of violence would be another way to stop them and I would be behind that threat." Although believing that inducing fear would be necessary if other tactics do not work, Vlasak said he would not carry out the violence himself.

Let's refocus the picture. The other animals of the world are deemed property, rightless beings.[9] Current statistics reflecting various forms of animal exploitation, from fur sales to milk consumption to genetic engineering, indicate that society has yet to accept the concept of animal rights, if it's on society's radar screen at all. If activists want to change the laws that hold other animals captive, they must first change the values of the community; yet violence has the reverse effect. The talk won't be mainly about whether we can ethically use animals for food, clothing, amusement, or experiments; it will be about whether people should accept change led by individuals who frighten others into refraining from lawful activities. Real change would only come from a serious discussion of the first question, but that will be an idea before its time until education is undertaken. Animal rights, like most emerging movements, is oft-ridiculed and misunderstood. A vocal few, insisting that anything goes, will increase the level of ridicule and misunderstandings, while guaranteeing that a number of socially aware people steer clear. Few want to be seen rushing to support unreasonable persons with no thought process or plan, persons who might be dangerous. Consequently the public stands by as the governments create a mire of laws that can have their agents in our underwear drawer any minute.

There is nothing illegal about activists pressuring a corporation through e-mails and phone calls. Indeed, "virtual sit-in" will be a category defined in Sage Publications' new *Encyclopedia of Activism and Social Justice*. But support understandably diminishes when such pressure is perceived as a warning that firebombs or vandalism of employees' homes – or even the homes of the general public – will be next.[10] And where full-blown violence ensues, the government will seize its advantage. During the same hearing in which Vlasak made the remarks about justifiable force, Republican senator James Inhofe announced plans to introduce legislation to grant federal officers still more authority to counter animal-welfare militancy.

Senator Inhofe, chair of this particular Senate committee, was doubt-less delighted by Vlasak's performance. It was Inhofe who had invited John Lewis, FBI deputy assistant director for counterterrorism, to speak earlier in the year on animal welfare and eco-militancy, thereby setting the stage for the widely reported pronouncement on the 18th of May 2005: "There is nothing else going on in this country...that is racking up the high number of violent crimes and terrorist actions."[11] Inhofe secured a post in the leg-islature more than a decade ago by the grace of petroleum, real estate and agribusiness funding. And Inhofe has been well served by environmental and animal-welfare militants. So has Ron Arnold, who has successfully liaised the "Wise Use" campaign with fundamentalist Christians to lobby for the opening of public lands, including National Parks and wildlife refuges, to grazing, drilling and mining, and who is thought to have coined the term eco-terror.[12] Arnold, who has said that the Wise Use movement's "goal is to destroy, to eradicate the environmental movement,"[13] warns that envi-ronmental activists will kill. Arnold asks – or, as Steve Best says, "rightly asks" – "What happens when the next generation comes along and gets tired that these arsonists, the ecoterrorists, aren't doing enough?"[14] As one commentator said of Inhofe and Arnold, "If acts of property damage in the name of environmentalism and animal rights didn't exist, they would have been wise to invent them."[15]

Yet just a few months before Vlasak's appearance before the Senate committee, Frank Lautenberg's mind seemed far more open. When John Lewis said that the FBI believed "[i]nvestigating and preventing animal rights extremism and eco-terrorism is one of the FBI's highest domestic priorities", the senator asked if the bureau would deem anyone who protested government policy a potential terrorist. "Right to Life? Sierra Club?" asked Lautenberg, who then declared "I'm a tree hugger."[16]

Why would any advocate for environmental awareness and the interests of animals want to make anyone eat those words?

We know the common individual explanations for an aggressive posture; they're fairly simple, and Vlasak's conduct probably warrants little analysis. Unfortunately, though, when people willing to express such attitudes are invited to speak at conferences, there are no boycotts, nor the faintest whiff of protest, so newcomers might believe this is the pose to strike. In one instance a news writer presented a consultation with an "animal liberationist" who claimed not even to like most animals, and then insisted that people must view cows, pigs, chickens, monkeys, rabbits, mice, and pigeons as family members, and finally condoned arson and supported "unequivocally" the idea of an animal abuser happening to get killed in the process.[17] The activist would eventually land a job in the animal protection sector. The biographical article and others like it are published just as enthusiastically on advocacy sites as they are on the sites of detractors.

In other words, no matter how blatantly obvious it is that their militancy is a gift to their critics, some activists just keep on giving. There will always be young people in search of adventure and acclaim, and, for a variety of reasons, there will be individuals willing to provoke them. But at the level of group thinking, it's hard to explain a community's agreement to shoot itself in the foot. It's well known now that speeches are made that justify and even glorify violence at a number of conferences convened by and for the "animal rights" community. Given that such speeches are routinely quoted and successfully used to fuel restrictions on activism, why does this continue?

Interwoven with any plausible explanation is ambivalence. The advent of animal-rights philosophy in a truly radical, egalitarian form would defy millennia of social conditioning – first directed to survival, later kept in place in industrial society by domination so systematic that most do not notice it any more than they notice the air they breathe from moment to moment. At the core – in the advocates – the inevitable tension between human empathy with other animals and all the social messages we've absorbed about our collective vulnerability to them is at its most dramatic.

The ambivalence is evident in the campaigns themselves. Advocates might know what they oppose, but they are less sure about a positive vision to replace it. The leading ideals seems to derive from an ancient argument: whether we ought to see biblical dominion over animals as domination or the (presumably) more benign stewardship. Coherent advocacy would necessarily challenge our habit of domesticating other animals; yet that's not what most advocates or groups do. They collect and they spend on heart-tugging campaigns that suggest animals should all be treated more like pets. This is true of high-profile sanctuaries, with their photos of celebrities kissing rescued farm animals, and it's true of the big advocacy groups, with their promotions that offer supporters cuddly seal toys and their campaigns to call pet owners "guardians," and it plays a part in the emotional viewpoint of militants, who come to the task with memories of childhood dogs and "Hugs for Puppies" campaign slogans, and who attract new members by juxtaposing angry words with photos of fluffy-white rabbits.

Today, young activists are led by big fundraising groups to believe that promoting animal rights can mean persuading their schools to try eggs from better-treated hens. The campus "animal rights" group at the University of Connecticut convinced its dining hall to try out Certified Humane Raised and Handled eggs. In February 2006 the campus newspaper, the *Advance*, explained: "Some students have been vocal in the pursuit of a dining facility that follows a 'farm-to-fork' philosophy, emphasizing humane treatment of animals and minimal processing." The banana bread is now lighter and fluffier, says the paper, and students "seem to be eating more eggs just to try them out."

By March 2006, the improved eggs were featured under the banner "Eggcellent News for Hens" in *VegNews*, a magazine carried by organic grocers. For anyone believing that animal advocacy is becoming more radical, the article "Year of the Egg" underscores just how conservative it's become. After lauding the nationwide student movement to push connoisseur-class eggs, the article quotes a campaigner from the national Humane Society asking Ben and Jerry's to "do the right thing": use cage-free eggs in their ice cream. The story offers no critical mention of ice cream, or the company's reliance on the processing of dairy cows and their offspring – veal calves. Because all of this is under the heading "Veg Report," the unspoken assumption is that people may choose between the products of animal agribusiness yet identify themselves as vegetarian without giving the ethics of the word serious thought. It's as though by paying more, that question is resolved. When industry concessions to campaigners become part of the expected course of business, we might even wonder if agribusiness adopts the most appalling habits just to have something to concede, so that they too can be praised in trendy magazines.

The stewardship model is also evident in the promotional literature for sanctuaries. Farm Sanctuary calls itself the nation's leading farm animal protection organization. Its *Legacy Society* enables bequeathers to "guarantee that your voice for farm animals carries on, until farm animals are protected from abuse forever." The group's "Adopt-A-Turkey Project" does not challenge the idea of domestication, but celebrates it. The charity's website tells of "adoptive parents," and "the deep bond that developed with their turkeys," and "how their feathered family members enriched their lives." A string of television personalities explain that farm animals make good pets. "Like cats and dogs," says Persia White, "Turkeys are intelligent, social, and sensitive beings who want to live." Charlotte Ross is pictured kissing a turkey, and Linda Blair claims, "Turkeys are misunderstood. Once I adopted turkeys, I understood this large bird to be a great companion. Contrary to popular belief, they are sweet, kind and funny. My adopted girls filled my heart every day with joy." The promotional page concludes, "Turkeys love cuddles, kisses and tickles just as much as people do!" and invites visitors to "click here for turkey love tales."

Treating farm animals as pets calls on us to delight in the total subservience expected by an affluent society over its animals. Indeed, the custom of petkeeping was established as a display of status by a population which can afford to keep more animals than it can use as food, with the leisure time to breed animals to enjoy as a form of play.[18]

Free-living animals are less discussed by advocates. Particularly conspicuous attacks on them, such as official expansions of hunts, are decried as "cruel" and "barbaric." Barbaric means foreign, alien, from *bar-bar*, the sound that Greeks thought foreigners made. But barbarism really isn't in the other, the weird, the shocking. It's in our everyday experiences, where we can and must begin to end it. By believing in superiority and inferiority, then by commodifying the living beings surrounding us, we've made ourselves foreign to the land. We've literally alienated ourselves from life.

A bear hunt might be triggered because people, lacking an understanding of bears' nature, get too close and personal with them until, not surprisingly, a dangerous encounter occurs. At this point, activists – people willing to be arrested in the woods on behalf of these animals – will describe them as "shy" and "magical," as though they were discussing teddy bears, thereby perpetuating the attitudes that caused trouble in the first place. New Jersey anti-hunting activists have even asked the governor to solve the bear problem by using experimental contraceptives on the animals. If they stop existing, bears won't be a nuisance. The activists seem willing to try any angle *except* explaining that dangers posed by free-living animals aren't a problem, but rather a risk, and a natural element of living fully on a healthy planet.

Alas, the hydraulic pull of donations and mainstream popularity has tamed activists, so that they, like the animals for whom they make their claims, don't challenge settled hierarchies and create risk. If campaigners got serious, they'd have to implicate their colleagues and partners. Question revered family traditions. Pause to reflect on the content of their refrigerators. That's the work of putting animal-rights theory into action; and it hasn't a thing to do with making threats or using force. It involves a commitment to avoid violence – a far more radical proposal.

Instead, activists use safe strategies borrowed from the corporate world. Social marketing, for example, which offers a moral good to the consumer who pays either with money or intangibles: time, effort, the risk of social disapproval. But not too much. Moral marketing conforms to the status quo by toning its message down, gaining adherents by advertising the benefits as being greater than the costs. It's the "easy sell" and it doesn't educate so much as offer a buffet of opportunities for the public to choose – the consumer's prerogative, after all – to avoid the moral imperative of respect for conscious beings. Few groups are willing to cultivate a public demand for peaceable, animal-free farming unabashedly. Activists ask people to eat less meat, tout companies that agree to inspections during slaughter, and praise burger restaurants that offer salads and soybean patties. Any corporation can be courted. Burger King experimented with a nearly vegetarian patty in the summer of 2002, and while small vegetarian restaurants struggled, the Burger King logo (a stylized picture of red meat between tan pieces of bread) appeared as a prominent pop-up advertisement on People for the Ethical Treatment of Animals' internet home page. The same group lavishly praised McDonald's for "groundbreaking improvements" in animal husbandry and slaughter.

Professionalized welfare advocacy thus largely functions to ensure that activists conform to the received social and economic template. Although "animal welfare" is the term most commonly known, perhaps the better term is husbandry, for what welfare charities largely seek is the sense that animals are used in society without undue suffering. True attention to an animal's welfare would not permit the fashioning of that animal into a commodity, let alone advertising companies that base their success on that paradigm. Rather than advance animals' basic interests, welfare lobbying agrees to elaborately codify the human right to use other animals, and commodified animals will always be rightless. That's what it means to be property.

Serious ideas about ensuring animals' freedom cannot emerge from non-profit bureaucracies that lobby, fundraise, and provide resources and expertise in care for animals used for (or no longer valuable to) commercial purposes. Throughout the advancement of bigger, better confinement and healthy, sustainable animals, free-living animals are continually pushed to the outermost edges of habitable terrain. Professional campaigners relegate animal rights to the margins of activism just as they relegate the animals who can have rights to the margins of the globe. While they focus on better confinement and preferred methods of slaughter, they let the interests of free animals languish and become invisible. Yet if free-living animals were thought to have a claim to their territory and freedom, then finally, finally, the polluting and resource-consuming ranchers and animal farmers would meet a true challenge!

It might seem surprising that militants also miss this point, but rescues and undercover exposures fit well with traditional ideas about extending measures of humane protection to animals. At their most dramatic, acts of rescue alight upon particularly harrowing conditions, providing sensational visual recordings of horrible cruelty and barbarism.

It's autumn 2003 and SHAC is sponsoring a finalist for Miss England. Jodie Lee praises masked rescuers and infiltrators, and declares, "My view: target the people who employ these disgusting animal murderers." Lee adds, "It's hard to look at my pets knowing that every day innocent animals are being tortured. I have had my two ponies for 9 years now, and I've grown up with them every day since I was 10 years old. To me, my ponies and I have such a special bond – unbreakable." Militants, too, know there's publicity value in heartwrenching sales of baby animals, the use of cramped cages and crates, long transport routes, and foreign habits. Popular with groups both militant and traditional is the notion that humane animal ownership can and should exist. But rare is the educator who weathers peer pressure to discuss the benefits of a daily philosophy that doesn't rely on dominating other animals.

A particularly striking example of militancy mixed right into a husbandry campaign comes from a South Australian advocate who sought formal permission to camp three weeks in a "modern commercial piggery." Ralph Hahnheuser hoped to attract the media to film the expected sores and sickness. Australia's *ABC News* did air Hahnheuser's claim that the pens are too small ("two metres long by 60 centimetres wide, with a concrete floor and no bedding"). The issue of pen size permitted reporters to entirely avoid the question of whether people should eat pigs.

Hahnheuser, who has run for a Senate seat in Australia, also wrote an open letter against shipping sheep "without routine veterinary supervision" and added that transporting live sheep "puts thousands of animals through such stress that they refuse to eat, and suffer and die on these filthy ships of shame" owned by "an industry that exports thousands of jobs and millions of dollars to countries that benefit from our stupidity, and then subject Australian animals to a cruel and brutal ritual slaughter." Although the letter protested ritual slaughter and decried benefits for non-Australians, it did not challenge the average Australian's own custom of consuming 37 pounds of sheep flesh in a year.[19]

Eventually Hahnheuser was prosecuted for (admittedly) adding pig flesh to food for sheep bound for Kuwait. Hahnheuser's lawyer said the act was done on behalf of the animals' welfare and not meant to cause an economic loss to those shipping them. The contamination dressed that uninspiring message in a militant cloak, and then drew invidious arguments about religion and culture into an issue that clearly implicates people of various cultures, including the activist's own. And, like earlier cases of sabotage by contamination, it raised public fears.[20] In 1984, a contamination hoax – a rat poison threat to protest dental research on monkeys, resulting in a recall of millions of Mars chocolate bars – was followed by a period in which pacifists distanced themselves from the ALF, and in which the media, once sympathetic, increasingly ignored animal-related activism or viewed it with alarm.[21] Should we call such methods direct action? They're actions, but how direct? They would be direct *if the deliberate goal were to repel or frighten many people*. In contrast, the basis of serious vegetarian outreach is an unwavering commitment to non-violence.

As for the pig pens, any campaign that focuses on space will be somewhat arbitrary. There is no correct area of confinement, so the activist will simply target the industry's minimum allowance. Animal agribusiness, whose profit is the foremost duty owed to shareholders, will always have its worst cases, its lamest animals, its smallest pens, its longest drives. Numerous corporations have agreed to work on ameliorating such cases, aware that stress can fuel illness and diminish quality control. After the negotiations with activists, a company can slap a seal of compassion on the product and use the agreement as a selling point. Increasingly, animal maintenance standards become corporate marketing tools. Serious attention to other animals' interests is not forthcoming from those who interact with them mainly by digesting them, and the advocates themselves don't ask for that serious attention. They indicate that a company deserves support when some other company's standards are worse. This is not advocacy, but a self-fulfilling expectation of failure. The world isn't going to become vegetarian overnight, goes the refrain; as though anyone who isn't "the world" wouldn't be worth asking, as though a movement for social change must promise overnight perfection.

This defeatism makes sense if advocacy for another's interests is viewed in tension with the whole, long history of a collective belief that we must compete with other animals rather than respect their interests. The communal resolution to compete with other animals is, quite arguably, what directs the competitive activist – the one who takes a side, the one who sees the task as a war – to lose.

"Right now we're in the early stages of World War III," says Paul Watson, who now directs the Sea Shepherd Conservation Society, a group founded to fight parties who kill or capture marine mammals. "We are the navy to Earth First!'s army," adds Watson, apparently forgetting that navies and armies, with their fire, napalm, Agent Orange, landmines, uranium, and released crude oil can devastate animal life as well as human health. Watson insists: "The environmental movement doesn't have many deserters and has a high level of recruitment. Eventually there will be open war."[22]

Some of the recruits might use the tough talk to chase off doubt and temptation. Animal advocates, especially newcomers whose knowledge of theory is minimal, will confess, from time to time, to being tempted to pick up a gooey, Chicago-style pizza or a latté from the local coffee bar – especially when these are part of their peers' social events. Some psychologists think that politically motivated violence helps ward off the temptation of the pleasures of the outer world. This happens when the attacker has a sense of being a victim or a martyr of the larger society. To the newcomer, according to this theory, "direct action" is direct because it immediately quashes personal ambivalence about a commitment perceived as a sacrifice. Appearing in court or submitting to a legal penalty publicly demonstrates one's commitment. Whether or not one gets caught, forcible actions reaffirm loyalty to the cause, while fending off the cruel people who represent the temptation to rejoin the society of childhood, a society where other animals are used, but where we remain comfortably unaware, as we unwrap cheese cubes from papers with pictures of laughing cows.

CHAPTER NINE

Charity is no substitute for justice withheld.

ATTRIBUTED TO AUGUSTINE OF HIPPO

No Barbarism, Please; We're Americans

Steven Best describes a new breed of freedom fighters that has "ditched Gandhi for Machiavelli" and is dedicated to animal liberation by any means necessary. Best calls it "a guerrilla war in which liberation soldiers disperse into anonymous cells, descend into the underground, maneuver in darkness, deploy hit-and-run sabotage strikes against property, and attempt to intimidate and vanquish their enemies." Adds Best, "'War' entails violence, hatred, bloodshed, and an escalation of conflict when dialogue fails." And the professor is ready to bring it on. Exhorts Best: "May the armies of the animal, Earth, and human liberationists rise and multiply in a perfect war against the oppressors of the Earth."[1]

The Activist as Superhero, whether speaking from an academic office or as a young rebel, thrives on the existence of an antagonist. Where there is no enemy, the Superhero creates one. The Superhero can then sling globs of cream pie, or bricks, firebombs, or threats, all for the idea of a greater good.

The Superhero misses what the creative organizer knows: The people we engage are us. They are our parents, our siblings, the people next door; they're the names in our address lists, they're our teachers, students, and co-workers. Whether we like to admit it or not, we're all the owning class. We are humanity, born in a world of stock markets and prisons, cyclones and extinctions, striving for recognition, for knowledge, or for spiritual growth, or all of this. If we're committed to social progress and have the strength to find out what it takes and ask for what we want, our potential is boundless. We're the existentialists who take courage in the words of the heavenly philosopher Quentin Crisp: We swim with the tide, but faster.

By declining to bargain with industries for small changes, we avoid being placated by temporary and illusory gains. We decline to celebrate confusion. We know that businesses and media are willing to present us as winning if the status quo is reinforced; and we aren't entertaining the offer. We know that exposing illegal cruelty satisfies the consensus that the use of animals can acceptably go on, managed and controlled and regulated, buttressing the image of a self-proclaimed advanced and caring populace as billions are served. We decline to extend tacit support to the view that progress means conquering nature, and animal use is normal, or noble, or eternal. To do less is to let the wheels of activism spin in the very mire we came to clear.

Nor is it enough to read animal-rights books and leave them on a shelf apart from the environmental casebooks, for environmental ethics is the natural home of a respectful view of other animals, if those animals are to be permitted to live where freedom is still possible, on their own terms. Seekers of animal rights must not settle for being steered off to commercial welfare pursuits: zoo animals, animals in labs, or those bred, fattened, killed, and processed on farms and in factories. Advocates' e-mail accounts quickly fill to the brim with alerts and commentary from people who study or manage other animals, and want to influence institutions. Add the urgent calls for rescues, and these messages can turn activists into collectors of stranded animals, or into analysts or enforcers of humane legislation, lacking environmental bearings. Not to be confused with animal-rights theory, the professional animal welfare paradigm is based on neither life nor liberty but rather the promotion of husbandry: caring for animals the way we'd care for rightless workers or inanimate machines. The Humane Society of the United States, in a column entitled "HSUS in Action," informs its members:

> *Our Rural Area Veterinary Services (RAVS) and Humane Society International (HSI) staff visited a dozen communities around Colán, Peru, and an ecological park in Piura during the 2006 working Equine Clinic. This is the fourth year we've held the clinic, and everything ran like a well-oiled machine. ...Our RAVS clinic taught farmers about hoof care for working horses, integral parts of the community.* [2]

The same page provides photos of horses and donkeys, their heads or necks in ropes, mouths being examined and hooves filed, as South American children watch.

We hear that the point of animal advocacy is to better the "human-animal bond" while reducing the suffering that humans impose on other animals. Much is made, then, of the mission of stirring compassion for animals. Compassion: to pity or suffer together. Oh, how dreary! The reduction of suffering, when it takes over as a mission, becomes, for the objects of this advocacy, a reduction *to* suffering. And this, too, misses animals on their own terms, for the lives and interests of other animals constitute something far more wondrous and more complex than the sum of harms to which we subject them.

Consider this commentary from the Friends of Animals brochure entitled "Who We Are":

> *Humans have imposed harnesses and saddles on wild horses and African wild asses for domestic work. Breeders have crossbred horses and donkeys, creating mules – capable of even more labor. But attempts to domesticate zebras, equids closely related to wild horses and wild*

asses, have met with utter failure. Africa's zebras have an unknown quality that defies domestication. Friends of Animals admires this "wildness" and seeks to protect it. With knowledge that we cannot control everything, we might learn to control ourselves.

Who we are, as animal rights advocates: We are people longing for a world where animals are permitted to live where freedom is possible, on their own terms. Air, earth, woods, water, wind, freedom…What are animal rights but the freedom to live on their own terms and not ours? The guiding principle here isn't to help them, but to aspire not to interfere.

That's not the same as doing nothing. Everywhere, roles wait to be creatively filled, and every day is an opportunity to teach and to learn. In this communication process, one of the first things to be discussed is that "helping animals" whether by illegal rescue or legal management is not just something that one does along the path to a distant animal-rights ideal. In reality, "helping animals" is usually the obstruction in the path.

Consider the helping of free-living animals by imposing artificial birth control. Few would argue against the idea of neutering domesticated pet animals; these animals are selectively bred to be dependent on humans. Because it's disrespectful to afford them an autonomy that's incomplete and not in their best interest, declining to create more dependent animals is the best decision an animal-rights activist can apply. A caretaking ethic will attend the relationship between a human and a beagle for as long as beagles are bred. But imposing contraception on groups of animals whose autonomy can realistically be respected is the application of human hegemony over animals who are living naturally, so that they then become controlled and contained by government agencies, humane groups, or private owners.

The Humane Society and the Bureau of Land Management collaborate on research, development, and application of contraception in wild horse populations.[3] The Humane Society holds an investigational new drug permit from the Food and Drug Administration to experiment with a contraceptive vaccine, and studies are underway on free populations of deer, elephants, bears as well. "Wild horses are an American treasure at risk because of drought conditions, competition for habitat, and pressures from the cattle industry to wipe them out," said Andrew Rowan, the Society's executive vice president. "Contraception offers the hope of maintaining a healthy herd and a well-balanced eco-system." The Humane Society's apparent willingness to conceive of engineered cattle,[4] deforestation, the denuding of ranges and riverbanks, and massive water pollution as part of a balanced eco-system is underscored by the description of itself as "committed to working with all stakeholders to develop and implement a viable plan to use this wildlife management tool to improve the welfare of wild horses." The welfare group's agreement to add another layer of control over the animals without disturbing their valuation as resources distinguishes animal welfare management from an animal-rights approach.

The Society has campaigned against the three plants which have operated in the United States for the purpose of slaughtering horses for human consumption. (The campaign does not denounce the slaughter of horses for other products commonly used in the United States, such as glue or gelatine.) Putting the theme of the campaign in the Society's own words, Dr. Rowan declares: "Americans are sickened by the thought that our wild horses could end up as someone's dinner in Belgium or Japan." The Bureau of Land Management points out that it still wants an overall reduction in numbers. The Society doesn't argue the point. Dr. Rowan simply says contraception will help ensure "that our horses are protected as a unique and valuable resource for future generations."

In addition to this complete negation of the interests of the horses for themselves rather than as a resource for unborn *Homo sapiens*, there's a certain smug nationalism here, unjustified, considering how routinely animals are slaughtered and eaten in the United States – and that wild horses and burros are removed because cattle owners want space to graze and process still more animals for slaughter. The Humane Society alerts manage not to mention the reason horses are ousted from the land is ranching, that to make every last raggedy spot of land over to cattle grazing, ranchers and government agents who support them continually move the horses and burros, and a great number of other undomesticated animals. So to say that "Americans are sickened" by what someone does in Belgium or Japan sounds less like honest public debate than pandering to xenophobia. Serious animal rights or environmental advocacy is made infinitely more difficult when advocates' rhetoric works against human tolerance, respect, and kindness, all the while deflecting serious thought about why the interests of animals matter. Slaughter continues – hold the barbarism.

The true question for advocates is why free-living horses and burros must be marched off the land, whether killed immediately, put into government holding pens, adopted into the cycle that results in slaughter later, or made to chemically disappear – all to augment the corporate wealth of ranch owners. Animal commodities can stay; animals who aren't commercially useful get hooked off stage. One form of disappearing might well be less gory than another, yet only by allowing room for discussion of domination itself can advocates spark serious change in thinking about the position of other animals.

A North Carolina legend had it that the criminal law would not interfere in marital violence as long as the battery did not involve a rod thicker than one's thumb; this notion is thought to be one possible origin of the phrase "rule of thumb."[5] A review of nineteenth-century case history shows that it's more likely that some people believed in the existence of a rule forbidding the use of a switch too thick to pass through a wedding ring.[6] Any customs or comments that limited the thickness of allowable rods, or the degrees of permitted injury, were doubtless thought to avert something barbaric; yet with the benefit of hindsight we know that such notions wouldn't forbid immoral action so much as allow it.

A view that the criminal law should limit the intensity of beatings only showed the pervasive cultural acceptance of domestic violence. Moreover, at its deepest and most insidious level, the allowance for a right of chastisement in marriage, no matter how carefully regulated by custom, defined female humanity as a subjugated class. Animal- welfare regulations and anti-cruelty laws are the animals' official rules of thumb. They accept, codify, and perpetuate assumptions that an enlightened populace will one day understand as morally unacceptable, as we acknowledge that egalitarianism, simple respect for the personhood of another, does not admit of degrees. One decides to think respectfully, or one does not.

By accepting and helping to carry out pharmaceutical experimentation, by continual involvement in the manipulation and control of animals, by tacitly agreeing that animals cannot possibly be left with their autonomy intact – No, they'll take over! – professionalized welfare advocacy upholds the consensus that animals simply must be kept in check if not used as food, clothing, entertainment, or objects of curiosity. That's society; it's not going to change in our lifetime, goes the objection, *so we're not going to be the ones changing it.*[7] In a striking parallel, militants object that education won't work in our lifetime, and they are going to do whatever they can to improve the situation – not fundamentally change it.

Employees of the campaign group International Fund for Animal Welfare, known as IFAW, have engaged in spectacular scuffles with residents of Canadian coastal regions, people who carry out the government-sponsored spring seal kill. Yet this same campaign group has been deeply involved for years in tweaking the Marine Mammal Regulations to align the practice with supposedly humane standards. When Canada's government issued its quota of seal kills for 2006, the Premier of Newfoundland and Labrador made comments that implied a link between IFAW and the FBI's domestic terror probes. Oddly, when demanding the politician's apology, IFAW's president publicly cited the group's previous assistance to the marine animal trade, pointing out that in the past year the group had leveraged some $1.2 million dollars, including $600,000 in U.S. government funding, to "assist New England fishermen with their animal welfare practices and provide them with state of the art fishing gear."

On its face, the campaign group's letter insists it can't seriously be deemed terroristic if it's working with the U.S. government. The subtext here says, "Leave us alone: For heaven's sake, we distributed supplies to the fish industry; can't you see we aren't challenging the status quo?" The letter establishes its mainstream credentials by going along with the routine, socially acceptable violence to animals and the marine ecology.[8] This dissonance is common, including in campaigns with the most aggressive posture against the seal kill.

The dissonance took the form of promotions for a "Canada seafood boycott": From the mainstream U.S. Humane Society to the Animal Liberation Front, welfare groups used marine animals as leverage by asking consumers to buy fish products from outside of Canada for so long as the Canadian government carried out the seal kill. One need not subscribe to the animal-rights position to note the likelihood that a temporary boycott of Canadian fish products would conclude by feeding the long-running cycle in Canada, in which depletion of cod and other marine life is decried, a reduction in seals is promoted to allow other marine life (and the coastal economy) to rebound, and the seal-killing resumes. But the Sea Shepherd Conservation Society promised to remove from the boycott list any Canadian fish traders that agreed to denounce the seal trade. And in April 2006, the North American Animal Liberation Press Office distributed a "Communiqué" from the Animal Liberation Front announcing that bomb threats were made against four Red Lobster restaurants, because the chain of fish restaurants declined to get involved in the boycott of Canadian marine products and therefore, according to the message, "Red Lobster continues to deal death on the ice" regarding "over 300 thousand seals clubbed to death this year in Canada."[9]

Out of hundreds, one further example of this mix of aggressive and staid groups promoting dissonant campaigns. As briefly mentioned in the last chapter, militant and mainstream welfare groups agreed, in the midst of a continuing debate over whether the state of New Jersey should hold bear hunts, that contraceptive chemicals would be an acceptable way to control bears. In an experiment run by the Humane Society at the Six Flags Wild Safari amusement park, veterinarians injected several bears with porcine zona pellucida, or PZP, a vaccine derived from pig tissue.[10] A local advocacy group grew impatient with these efforts, and pushed for the use of Neutersol, a chemical castration product developed for dogs. But no studies had been done to determine dosages for any animals except puppies, and even the developers of Neutersol were taken aback by the activists' desire to use a lot of it and see if it would work on bears. The New Jersey Animal Rights Alliance (a group which, perfectly aligned with the militant welfare pattern, supports Animal Liberation Front rescues and campaigned to close a zoo which, the group's director pointed out, repeatedly violated the federal Animal Welfare Act) offered to put up $10,000 to cover the testing, with the aim of sterilizing 100 bears. The campaigners, much like the people who were demanding a hunt, saw bears as their problem to solve. There's little room in the whirlwinds of these desperate initiatives to talk about why we humans might be better advised to accept that risk is part of living in a vibrant ecology.

Although most animal advocates have yet to become active ecologists, ecologists have begun to think seriously about animals, and that's creating an intriguing sphere of thought and action. Environmentalists decry animal activists – often with good reason – for focusing on "charismatic" beings rather than an integrated biocommunity; and yet arguably, only by cultivating a respect for conscious individuals living in their habitat can environmentalists transcend fetishism. The natural world has no interests in its own health; it's the conscious life within it for whom its health has meaning.

Nearly three decades after David Ehrenfeld asked if people are "ready to move beyond humanism"[11] it's entirely respectable for environmentalists to propose the idea that inherent worth was not bestowed by nature upon the human species alone, and environmental law writers are increasingly willing to perceive non-human animals as more than simply part of the legal landscape. As Dale Goble and Eric Freyfogle point out, "[e]nvironmental law, once focused on direct threats to human health, now is concerned with assaults on non-human life".[12] Ecologists and, in turn, people who make decisions about water and land are questioning the assumption that nature is merely a big source of material value. And insofar as it offers material value, they're suggesting that the value be shared with animals striving to meet their most basic needs and interests.

We're ready to grow up as a species. We've developed a way of perceiving other beings, not as toys or objects to bring us pleasure; not as food commodities; but as beings with their own experiences of the natural world. We're seeing ourselves as part of the greater biocommunity, and we should expect the new generation of "animal lawyers" to get out of the management mode and reflect this vision.[13] Law that's at home with natural laws, a simple recognition of the environment as home to other, morally important beings, will represent a sea change. Indeed, to pry the hand of legal control from the necks of other animals and to focus on controlling ourselves in relations to them would help restore the seas to the health they had before we thoughtlessly changed them.

CHAPTER TEN

*All violence, all that is dreary and repels,
is not power, but the absence of power.*

RALPH WALDO EMERSON

Draconian Activism

George Svokos decided to bring his complaints about threatening calls and stolen mail to the New Jersey courts.[1] The filings report that someone broke into the Svokos home, took a credit card and racked up $5,000 in charges, including on an order for home delivery of a blow-up sex doll. Svokos is president of the drug-marketing company Plantex USA, whose parent company, Teva Pharmaceuticals, uses a laboratory run by Huntingdon Life Sciences.

Campaigners, the lawsuit reported, also accused Svokos of inappropriate contact with children.[2] The militant website *Bite Back* published unsigned correspondence which mentions Svokos's connections with Teva, from parties who "contacted the pastor, secretary, and several parishoners [sic] at St. Nicholas Greek Orthodox Church, which Plantex-USA President George Svokos and his wife are members of." The message also states, "We told them that we were a parishoner [sic] and that we and a couple others had observed George inappropriately watching and touching young children, and asked the pastor to intervene before we had to call the police."[3] A temporary injunction separated picketers from the Svokos residence.

Over three thousand miles away in the village of Newchurch, in central England, lives the Hall family. Christopher and John Hall manage Darley Oaks farm, which, for a number of years, supplied animals to Huntingdon Life Sciences. At Darley Oaks, campaigners said, animals bred for biomedical experiments lived in appalling conditions, allegations the family denied. The Save the Newchurch Guinea Pigs campaign included peaceful vigils, but also resulted in the Halls' phone lines being jammed by hundreds of calls, and the deliveries of piles of unwanted mail-order items. The campaign spread out against the whole village, and involved abusive graffiti, bricks thrown through windows, cars paint-stripped, phone lines cut off, and explosives let off at night.[4] Effigies were burned. May Hudson, a cleaner, was warned that her dead husband would be disinterred unless she stopped working for the Halls. Hudson quit after her children and grandchildren received threats. One worker had his name spelled out with shotgun cartridges on his lawn and left after death threats were made against his grandmother. The Hall's local pub received warnings that its beer would be poisoned. When companies that collected milk from the Halls' dairy cattle stopped coming, the family started selling the cows. Rod Harvey, manager of small fuel delivery service with a stop at Darley Oaks, had never seen the guinea pigs; but a letter was circulated, accusing Harvey of being a paedophile. A golf club threw the Halls out after greens were dug up.

Gladys Hammond was the mother-in-law of Christopher Hall, the farm's co-owner. Hammond passed away in 1997, at the age of 82, and was buried at an old country churchyard, St. Peter's, in the village of Yoxall. In October 2004, someone unearthed the coffin and carried Hammond's remains away.[5] Only a jawbone was left at the grave; the jaw, and the knowledge that Hammond had been buried with a grandchild's soft elephant toy, would be known to the police and to those responsible for digging up the body and employing it as a bargaining tool.[6] Letters arrived at Chris Hall's home, demanding a stop to the breeding of guinea pigs in return for the bones. The Florida-based website of the militant magazine *Bite Back* hailed the bodysnatching as a successful act of sabotage; the site had also published an Animal Liberation Front message stating, "Guinea pig killer John Hall loves his daughter very much! He would have been devastated to hear then that a crucified voodoo doll containing 70 skewers plunged into every orifice and with the eyes and mouth cut out had been left on his daughter's doorstep in the dead of night! Get it straight John Hall: your cameras mean nothing, prison time means nothing, your money means nothing - YOU CANNOT STOP US!"

When letters claiming to come from the Animal Rights Militia announced that one sixth of the remains of Gladys Hammond were buried locally, in a plastic container two feet under the 90-acre Brackenhurst Woods, a hundred police fanned out over the vast area, searching in vain. Chris Hall said demonstrators turned up outside their home after the bodysnatching incident to chant verbal abuse at them. "It shows the kind of people they are," said Hall. "It shows what sort of world we are forced to live in."

All over the world, people could see news photographs of the churchyard, with its gravesite surrounded by police tape. And what would unfold, more clearly than ever before, was the terrible conflict within activism, between the hunger strikers and the bodysnatchers. The latter had become what they despised. Tearing at the social fabric in order to promote a cause has been seen in right-wing interest groups – other circles that attract easily manipulated joiners. In some areas of the central United States, laws now require demonstrators to keep a certain distance from military funerals, in response to the fundamentalist Westboro Baptist Church of Topeka, whose congregants turn up at soldiers' funerals to preach the gospel by shouting hateful phrases and holding signs that read "Thank God for IEDs" – improvised explosive devices. Roadside bombs, church members say, are God's punishment to soldiers who defend a nation that tolerates homosexuality.

A number of activists condemned the theft of Hammond's remains; but to some it seemed that the intimidation had worked, for it was less than a year later, in the summer of 2005, that the Halls announced they would wind down their guinea pig breeding venture. The announcement came with a plea: "We hope that, as a result of this announcement, those responsible for removing Gladys's body will return her so she can lie once again in her rightful resting place."[7] Around 200 campaigners rallied for a victory celebration.[8]

Anyone could have predicted the effect of a victory march just four miles from Newchurch would have on the local community. The scene was the focus of the British media. The activists' parade followed a public appearance by the Archdeacon of Walsall, photographed on bended knee beside the desecrated grave, begging for the return of the remains. In such circumstances, the parade was seen an insensitive at best, a condonation of the bodysnatching at worst. More than 50 officers, presumably some who had been sent to the woods in a futile search for the remains, hovered at the scene. Locals pelted the parade with bacon and eggs. An elderly observer called the marchers terrorists. To the extent that anyone credited victory to intimidation, the missing point was that such things are setbacks, not advancements. There is no victory in changing someone's conduct because a grave has been desecrated, or that they've been accused of molesting children.

If "radical" means "of the root," then radical animal rights advocates are people who work at the roots of oppression. Radical animal rights theory seeks a relationship with the world in which domination is utterly absent, a relationship ever so rare, and now everywhere surrounded by the great weight of millennia of hierarchical thinking. In contrast, it's not rights activism, but a steely utilitarian philosophy that supports ends-justified manipulation of others. The grave desecration simply adds itself to the everyday heap of coercion. It says the activists think the way to fix problems is to dominate, without comprehending that domination itself is what created the problem. In the quest to vanquish some mythical other side, the Newchurch campaign is might-makes-right all over again, with militant activists only serving to help spin the wheel. And so it was that four protesters were soon charged with conspiring to blackmail the Hall family with the grave desecration. One major paper wrote of the government's response to Newchurch this way: "Responding to draconian activism, government unveils new anti-ter-ror bill."[9]

By April 2006, with Gladys Hammond's remains then missing for a year and a half, three people faced twelve years in jail each, and a fourth faced up to six years, after admitting conspiring to blackmail the owners of Darley Oaks farm over a six-year period.[10] One had the registrations of cars of the Halls' relatives and of Peter Clamp, a councillor who tried to have activists banned from the area. Police also seized a photocopy of an anatomy book containing images of a human skull missing the lower jaw.

The punishments the activists faced were considered harsh. By com-parison, a person who deliberately goes out with a knife, carrying it as a weapon, and uses it to cause death, can expect to receive on conviction in a British court a sentence in the region of ten to twelve years.[11] The police suggested that the judge might shorten the sentence for any arrestee willing to divulge the location of the grandmother's remains, and in May 2006, just days before sentencing, an arrestee called John Smith told detectives where to look. As dog-walkers and elderly visitors stopped and stared, television viewers looked on, and a helicopter hovered overhead, police forensic teams in boots, gloves, and white paper suits recovered the remains about 14 miles from the churchyard, amongst the fir trees at the edge of a German war cemetery.[12] Detective Chief Inspector Nick Baker told reporters that Hammond's family members had been notified and were receiving the support and services of a police family liaison officer.[13] John Smith, who got twelve years after all, showed a raised-fist salute to supporters in the gallery.[14]

As for the company and whatever it did with the guinea pigs, well, few details were explored. Huntingdon Life Sciences goes on performing tests for drug companies, food industries, and agribusiness, albeit mainly by moving repeatedly out of the protesters' way. In 2001, a militant activ-ist clubbed managing director Brian Cass outside his home in England; and subsequently, believing that looser reporting standards in the United States would make it harder for SHAC to identify and target shareholders, Huntingdon removed its headquarters from Cambridgeshire to New Jersey.

And while an animal advocate named Steve Christmas lay in an intensive care unit after being deliberately run over by a hunter, Brian Cass was able to return to work the day after the attack.[15] From a human interest point of view the disparity in coverage was odd; but given Cass's financial profile, it was predictable.

In a suburb of London, in the summer of 2005, the Kendall family was startled by a nighttime explosion in their carport. Michael Kendall's employer, Canaccord Capital, quickly announced it would cut ties with a company named Phytopharm. Phytopharm had previously collaborated with Yamanouchi Pharmaceutical Company on an experimental Alzheimer's treatment, and Yamanouchi, in turn, was known for working with Huntingdon. Canaccord vowed to continue brokering for the biotechnology industry.[16]

"If you support or raise funds for any company associated with HLS we will track you down, come for you and destroy your property by fire," said the Animal Liberation Front's website, as reported to the world through New York's *Bloomberg News*. "An increasingly indiscriminate campaign," said London's *Guardian*, "has fanned from a variety of firms and people with any business or service ties to Huntingdon to those who have no links to HLS or animal testing." In June 2005, a Leicestershire truck driver came home to ALF graffiti and a home-made firebomb. It was a year and a half earlier that a pharmaceutical company's lawyer lived in the house.

Employees of testing firms do know they might be targeted, and they are quickly frightened by crank calls, property damage, or false accusations of crimes. The rising costs of protecting them, as well as protecting cement suppliers and so forth, have obstructed projects to build primate laboratories in Britain. One company sold its 11 percent stake in Huntingdon after a bomb scare at its London offices and the on-line distribution of its directors' home phone numbers. In December of 2002, the British government covered Huntingdon Life Sciences with emergency insurance when the world's largest insurance broker, Marsh & McLennan, quit after spending millions on security.[17] By the end of February 2003, a mere month's campaign of intimidation, including vandalism at the homes of employees, ended Huntingdon's relationship with auditing giant Deloitte & Touche. The campaign has also caused the company to lose accounts with Merrill Lynch, The Bank of America, the Bank of New York, and Goldman Sachs. Huntingdon left London's stock exchange; and in September 2005, the New York Stock Exchange unexpectedly delayed the company's listing just an hour before it had been scheduled to take effect, prompting questions from reporters worldwide. But if the actions of the militants appear to work on some level, it's neither the level of changing minds nor laws. Indeed, on both counts, they've triggered a fierce backlash.

Prime minister Tony Blair cited the grave desecration when signing an online "People's Petition" set up by the Coalition for Medical Progress, whose listed members include the Biosciences Federation, the Association of the British Pharmaceutical Industry, GlaxoSmithKline, Huntingdon Life Sciences, Pfizer, and Novartis, and whose stated role is "to help explain the case for medical progress and the benefits brought about by animal research."[18] As for the laws, licensing a typical new drug requires the use of an estimated 3000 nonhuman testing subjects, and animal experiments are going on in Britain at the highest rate in a decade, with 2.79 million experiments performed in 2003.[19] Singapore and China are attracting new clients for the laboratory work they offer – China at low costs, Singapore with promises of a protest-free environment. As for changing minds, the situation seems bleak.[20] "If SHAC activists seek to illuminate the condition of laboratory animals," wrote the *Boston Globe* in an August 2002 editorial, "they have failed. Their own tactics reveal a disturbing willingness to inflict suffering."

A friend of mine, a New York City activist, recalled:

It's been in the way of our work here for a long time. Last winter, at a department store vigil held by Caring Activists Against Fur, when any fur-clad woman appeared, a prominent person in the group would shout: Fur hag! You look disgusting! You're a monster! *The hostility increased when any of the passersby responded.*

The activist was wearing a full-length "baby-coat" with dozens of baby dolls stuck all over the coat to represent fur pelts. If I thought she looked bizarre, I can't begin to imagine what the person on the street thought. That animal-rights activists hate people, I supposed, and that the one with the loudest voice was speaking for all of us.

An older man, identified as her boyfriend, shouted insults. I remember looking around and seeing some in the group – women – looking very uncomfortable. After talking with some of them, I decided to have a conversation with the loud activist and tell her that she was upset-ting me and some others. She waved me off. I've been doing this for a long time, and the nice approach doesn't work; the only way to get through to fur-wearers is to make them fearful of wearing fur in public. *Walking between vigil sites, this activist yelled at a woman:* You should be ashamed! *The offending coat was obviously a leopard-print design, that's all. The woman wearing it explained that it wasn't fur, and the activist replied that the woman looked like a couch in it, and others in the group joined in, laughing and mocking the woman.*

So I distanced myself from the group, but it happened again at the Museum of Modern Art, where a young activist went up to a woman wearing fur and shouted Murderer! *at the top of his lungs, inches from her face. This young man has since become a devoted campaigner for WAR – Win Animal Rights. That moment stuck in my mind: the rage and hate, and how it must have felt to be on the other end of that.*

Speaking of the November 2005 "Fur-Free Friday," the *New Yorker* recalled a similar scene:

A man behind me shouted at a pair of women: "That fur makes you look

fat!" I turned and told him to please stop. Again, the angry reaction:
Being nice doesn't work; at least those women will be embarrassed.

When you learn about the reality of the fur industry, it is hard not to also get angry at the people who buy and wear it. But most people will listen to a kindly spoken message. How does a movement made mostly of women tolerate, let alone embrace, patterns of abuse?

And those with the loudest voices attract attention to themselves worldwide. In late 2002, as supermodel Gisele Bündchen paraded for the audience at a Victoria's Secret fashion show, anti-fur activists clambered onto the runway, brandishing signs that said "Gisele: Fur Scum." Bündchen was targeted for deciding to work with a mink company. The demonstrators either failed to notice or did not care that the show they interrupted had Bündchen wearing leather, not fur. Indeed, the model was scarcely wearing anything at all; the entire appearance traded flagrantly on sexual objectification; and here came the activists, holding "scum" labels behind the model, for a photo that went out to the world. The Reuters report suggested that Bündchen, "wearing a flamenco beaded miracle bra and a leather skirt over her thong," showed no emotion, but that the audience cheered as security nabbed the protesters.

The action could be written off as a mutually gratifying publicity stunt for the activist group and the thongmongers. Still, its willingness to ignore social context and the humanity of its target is telling. Activism has reached a low ebb when it opts for depersonalization over the cultivation of ideas, and prosecutors can stand in court, too, and read correspondence between strangers beginning with the words "Dear Scum."[21]

While a few high-profile spokespeople continue to argue that hostilely targeting animal use is somehow expedient, most concede that they've ditched their moral compasses and are playing by what they perceive as the enemy's rules.

Where enterprises start to appear seriously threatened by force, those rules will become most severe. In October 2003, as London's High Court passed out permanent injunctions to control campaigners, Tony Blair was assisting in the creation of a National Extremism Tactical Co-ordination Unit to manage activists. The government pointed to the public interest in the development of new drugs and treatments; yet its customary role as the protector of business unquestionably comes into play. Britons are frequently reminded that drugs make up a prized manufacturing sector. So, since the summer of 2005, unlimited fines and five-year sentences can be imposed, under the Serious Organized Crime and Police Act, upon someone who causes "economic damage" to pharmaceutical companies.

The Act has also allowed the police to operate on the cumulative effect of incidents. By focusing on the concept of conspiracy rather than holding themselves to the traditional legal duty of finding the direct perpetrators of crimes, the British and U.S. governments continue gradually augmenting their authority to curtail the activities of computer users who – stopping short of traditional illegalities such as direct incitement of violence – identify and publish personal details about targets, list actions that could intimidate them, and report the deeds of those who try. The British law has been steadily evolving to curtail protests in residential areas that cause alarm or distress and to enable companies to be deemed victims of harassment. The Home Office has also banned several U.S. militants from entering Britain for defending or advocating violence in speeches or writings, and in August 2005 created the Exclusion Bill to grant the state wide latitude to bar non-citizens who do so.

Reuters raised the volume by reporting a security analyst's characterization of Britain as "the Afghanistan of animal rights extremism."[22] By then, after complaints from the pharmaceutical sector about the scarcity of arrests, the Home Office had proposed yet another anti-terrorism bill, applicable to animal-welfare militants as well as al Qaeda supporters.[23] The new bill, which includes provisions to hold suspects without charge for 90 days, is intended to rein in campaigners who glorify or commit "violent acts of terror" to promote activism.

To press others to agree with forcible methods, activists sometimes equate the use of animals with the Holocaust, and the exploiters of animal bodies with Nazi figures. Hitler, in quintessentially utilitarian style, encouraged people to abandon their inhibitions in order to carry out any actions needed to achieve a goal; and, as Holocaust psychologist Richard Koenigsberg has explained, those who hesitated to go along with official policy faced indignation and rage, and were themselves accused of being oppressive or harmful to the nation. "We may be inhumane," Hitler declared, "but if we rescue Germany we have performed the greatest deed in the world."[24] The view that rescue justifies all forms of harm proved itself a bankrupt philosophy then, and so it is today. Its moral emptiness fuses the self-certitude of scientists using conscious beings who can't consent, and that of activists who oppose that use.

And as we've previously seen, those who see violence as efficient are quite often also willing to promote pragmatic ideas for reforming institutional use, yet call it a way forward to the abolition of that use. Thus, militants move to erase serious rights theory from the debate by incorrectly claiming that they apply it. And while reform movements have long showcased agreements with fast food outlets, zoos, research administrations, and so forth (claiming, depending on the audience, that the agreements had something to do with abolitionist intent or were only meant to ensure proper husbandry), the situation has worsened as animal welfarism has become militant animal welfarism. Now, corporations and their legislative backers must be fought by activist "combatants." Now, we hear that "collateral damage" is acceptable, for this is a war.

One writer in London's *Guardian* seized upon the paralepsis, that coy contrivance whereby one makes a statement by first declaring that one won't: "No one, I think, would put the attempt to liberate the Newchurch guinea pigs on a par with the anti-apartheid campaign in South Africa."[25] The writer forged ahead, recounting Mandela's guerrilla training in Algeria, Mandela's interest in properly controlled violence – a phrase, the writer explained, that's "perfectly appropriate for the things that animal rights activists have been doing to the Halls, their friends, families, employees and neighbours." Digging up the body of Gladys Hammond, then, is a "very precisely calibrated act of terror" which got its result and indeed was the only alternative for activists who would "stay true to their ideals". In the future, the writer continued, our treatment of other animals might be thought of as one of our great errors, and on that day the campaign "will surely look like a violent, necessary and ugly step on the long march to freedom."

Ultimately, assuming that we haven't damaged the web of life irreversibly, it is indeed likely that our treatment of other animals will be thought of a great moral error.

But so will our treatment of other humans, including the residents of Newchurch.

The victory statements equate success with a village's fear of protesters. How? If some activity only stops where and when people are terrified of force, what exactly has been advanced? Were animals vindicated, or simply replaced? The British media had reported that alternative animals for the testing industry had already been secured by the time the Halls announced their decision to stop breeding guinea pigs. Moreover, the Halls only resolved to stop one type of animal use, and as the farm's emphasis returns to dairy production, its business will use animals merely for the market of culinary pleasure.

It's unsurprising that activists have largely been quiet about the Halls' traditional farming operation. People who saw a victory in Newchurch believed that the sabotage was just, that extreme measures are appropriate tactics when decades of pleading, protest, and economic damage have failed. But thoughtful advocacy has not failed. In reality, a sustained, organized animal-rights initiative is just beginning to unfold. Although the term "vegan" is coming into its own, an animal-rights advocacy that's based on everyday living has been avoided by many of the mainstream advocacy groups, so that to date, less than 1% of the population has committed to vegan living. So the education is just beginning. It's premature to say that economic pressure has failed. It has barely begun.

No one among us can be arrested for buying eggless noodles. Yet setting ourselves free from the social addiction to animal products is serious direct action. The nitty-gritty of a movement is not a matter of decrying things that those people do – the terrible abuses, the torture photos of animal commerce – but of challenging, and then transcending, the violence of the everyday.

War-like activism, on the other hand, fits symbiotically with the cycle of social control, for it entails forcing someone to act in a certain way "because I said so," and the police soon have enhanced job security, and they will visit authoritarian tactics upon campaigners.[26] This ensures that everybody emerges with no individual soul-searching and no real change. Under enormous pressure and the threat of jail time, some arrested campaigners will agree to co-operate with the police, be classified as snitches, and find their former allies attempting to terrify them more relentlessly than any police force. As one publication put the point:

> *It is up to all of us to create an atmosphere that is not just unwelcoming– but hostile – to those who assist authorities in putting activists behind bars. We have to make the consequences for snitching more painful than potential jail time; until that time, we will have traitors in our midst.*[27]

And potential jail time will be daunting. More anti-terror laws will emerge to handle the eco-terrorist or, as more kind-hearted writers put it, eco-radicals. Strange how the word radical is deemed synonymous with violence, "direct action" with intimidation. As though peaceful work were not radical! As though eschewing the products of dominion were not direct action! And as though, in a movement for deep social change, only those whose displays of aggression make them vulnerable to state control, and the control of their nervous peers, are radical. Offering oneself up to the prison industry supports the makers of cages.

Campaigners rarely put their objections to vivisection into context by critiquing the paradigm that defines one class of living beings as the controllers and consumers of the rest. Even where agribusiness is discussed, the subject of dairy products is often relegated to a position of lesser importance or ignored. The Animal Liberation Front requires its activists to drop meat, but not milk. The arbitrary nature of that distinction emerges when domesticated animals are understood as beings within a whole system of human entitlement. The cream in the coffee might seem, to some, beneath the notice of activists, but the milk of the mothers of others is a good place to begin to question our universal domination of other conscious beings – indeed, the idea of domination itself. In the cream, we see the experience of a cow whose life consists of pregnancies and separations and whose death is violent, and if animal-rights activism means anything, it involves that cream. Donald Watson expressed this as clearly as it's ever been said, when recounting an early memory of visiting the animals on an uncle's farm:

> *They all "gave" something: the farm horse pulled the plough, the lighter horse pulled the trap, the cows "gave" milk, the hens "gave" eggs and the cockerel was a useful "alarm clock;" I didn't realize at that time that he had another function too. The sheep "gave" wool. I could never understand what the pigs "gave," but they seemed such friendly creatures ... always glad to see me. Then the day came when one of the pigs was killed: I still have vivid recollections of the whole process – including the screams, of course.*[28];

The child who would grow up to found a movement decided that farms – and uncles – had to be reassessed.

Chapter Eleven

*They defend their errors
as if they were defending their inheritance.*

Edmund Burke

Humanity:
An Alternative Performance

Our supremacy over other animals is interwoven with all of the hierarchies we've constructed to negotiate the world. Turning animals into commodities followed constraining and taming and learning to manipulate reproduction and breeding. Do we have it within us to try another paradigm?

In 1998, a widely printed news article called bonobos "the feminist apes."[1] Bonobos live in an obscure area of the Congo River basin, and, lucky for them, scientists didn't seem to notice them until the 1970s. (Once discovered, they became laboratory and zoo specimens.) Bonobos – who, scientists have said, are just as related to humans as to chimpanzees – challenge theories that the pattern of human evolution is inseparable from aggressive competition. They resolve social tension not through force, threats, or fights, but with sexual contact. They have been noted for their ability to view the world from someone else's perspective, and thus have been the subjects in some of the best-known examples of altruism in the non-human sphere. And although evolutionists had pictured early human society as resembling that of chimpanzees, which, in turn, they commonly describe as hierarchical and controlled by war-like males, primatologist Frans de Waal has said that "[w]e may be more bonobo-like than we want to admit."[2]

Hold on a minute, Frans. Not only would I want to admit it; I'd like to celebrate it. Drawing a bright line between the human species and the rest of conscious life, rather than acknowledging a continuum, has obstructed the expansion of our moral sphere. It's hindered us from learning from those outside that sphere. Finding patterns of co-operative relationships in other animal networks, and acknowledging that we could evolve emotionally by respecting their members rather than capturing, dominating, training, and experimenting on them, could mean developing the altruism that guides us to a truly civil society, saving ourselves and the living beings clinging to the lifeboat we call Earth.

Can we live non-hierarchically? We know that humans do change ideas about which groups ought to be dominated, and who comprises such groups. Noel Ignatiev observes the fluidity of dominance: The Irish moved, in the nineteenth century, "from being members of an oppressed race in Ireland to being members of an oppressing race in the United States."[3] Over time, declares Ignatiev, the Irish became white. Not by physical appearances; the transition, Ignatiev says, happened entirely in people's minds.

To overcome Protestants' resistance to extending civil rights, Ignatiev explains, the Irish both subjugated and dissociated themselves from people of African descent. And in this way, they succeeded in changing the membership rules of the white social club. At birth, people are "enrolled in that club without their consent or permission," and then "go through life accepting the rules and accepting the benefits of membership, without ever considering the costs." If they would flout and transcend the rules of conformity, Ignatiev posits, people would zero in on class issues, "which would open the door for all sorts of social and political changes that haven't happened yet, largely because some people settle for being white rather than take a chance on being free."

If we define "class" to mean *any position in an oppressive hierarchy*, then we can begin to transcend that structure rather than to obey the rules of yet another form of it.

Before developing a systematic horticulture, nomadic humans gathered most of their food for immediate use. As observed by anthropologist Donna Hart, we were more concerned with avoiding becoming prey than with hunting others. Prior to becoming rudimentary farmers, it's unlikely that we formed systematic gender hierarchies. Gradually, while absorbed in agrarian and animal domestication and confinement, we and our religious imagery became patriarchal. The moment of this changeover is not known precisely; author Elizabeth Fisher places it about 9000 years ago.[4]

The cultures of people who preserve ancient ways in the world today would suggest that there probably was no ancient matriarchy. The gathering society was fairly egalitarian, and property was largely held in common. Food was distributed to everyone in the tribe; support was mutual; and declining to participate was unthinkable.[5]

Still, as male humans don't bear children, they've been assigned other dangerous tasks, roles imbued with prestige, probably in order to motivate male humans to accept them. Part of striving for egalitarianism is understanding that the glorious or spectacular roles were often made that way to mask the vulnerability or expendability of those assigned them. In other words, we can get over ourselves. If we can define "class" to mean any position in a deliberately maintained hierarchy, then we can begin to transcend the entire repressive structure. That may well begin with acknowledging, just as childbirth is no longer magic, dangerous activity is no longer glorious; and war, along with most mechanisms for systematic depersonalization, is born of fear.

Many peace workers, environmentalists and social justice advocates integrate consensus methods into their work. They believe that the means of achieving change is part of change itself, and of creating the world they envision. And they have solid precedent. The Muscogee (Creek) people have the oldest political institutions in North America, with over four centuries of recorded history.[6] If consensus on a major issue could not be achieved to everyone's satisfaction, Muscogee people were free to move and set up their own community with the support of the town they were leaving. Consensus-based societies have also worked in guilds and in town councils. Christiania, an autonomous district in the city of Copenhagen, has been self-governed by its inhabitants using consensus since 1970. This encompasses decisions about cultural and educational issues, trade, water and electricity supply, health and security. Within the co-operative movement many residences and businesses employ non-hierarchical models, and even successfully apply them to complex financial decisions. If it all sounds utopian, in reality, it means working one day at a time, with patience and willingness to accept that we can achieve what we can imagine.

Freeing up our professionals from their corporate numbness would make perfect sense if their energies are to be directed to their best potential, socially and personally. We assume it's not utopian to want to eat anything produced on ever larger swaths of land, to order our food at the touch of a keyboard, to cure every disease, to live without pain, perhaps to live forever. These desires are utopian in the most unrealistic sense. They won't have a chance of actually leading to a utopia.

Of course, it takes time to unlearn the patterns of interacting that we've been brought up to accept as the norm. Unravelling our hierarchies would be a revolution more profound than anything in our modern memory. It would mean giving up the human clubs of whiteness, of maleness, and even of humanness, kicking the habit of defining ourselves as possessors of dominion over all that fly, walk, swim, and crawl over the contours of a weary planet.

It would mean the most comprehensive peace movement ever known.

The way out is via the door.
Why is it that no one will use this method?

Confucius

Epilogue

Animal rights is fundamentally about justice. Seeking justice as fairness and offering charity are not logically incompatible – at times, charitable responses are needed and welcomed – but it's important not to confuse these offerings with fundamental fairness, or to give up on that goal.

If we focus our energies on reducing the harms within a given institution – even if we do so while calling it a way forward to the abolition of use – then our activism is, in practical effect, indistinguishable from traditional charity. Coming to respect the interests of conscious beings in living on their terms does not mean seeking to erase all the suffering and risk that life involves. Such seeking misses the point of animal rights, seen in its best light.

On the other hand, insofar as harm is defined as the wide variety of insults and injuries visited upon conscious beings by the one group that has dominated the rest, and visited as part of that domination, then harm prevention is an integral part of animal-rights theory and action. It's not easy to measure the concrete results of a theory that seeks to transcend dominion, rather than modify the conditions of use. But we can see types of commodification ruled out completely, and ruled out for the express reason that they're oppressive. Most significant is the presence of individuals who commit, as far as possible, to live according to the idea. The more people we see developing such a commitment, naturally the more likely we are to find oppressive institutions phased out and creative ways of living designed in their place.

Animal advocacy, in recent years, has experienced two major setbacks, both forged in its own household. One is the idea that animal-welfare charities are compatible with radical change. The other is the idea that the use of force is a necessary or acceptable means of achieving that change. Both will continue to obstruct animal rights until they are acknowledged as obstructions and unequivocally challenged and addressed.

In reality, the animal-welfare concept, which seeks to ameliorate the worst conditions of use rather than question a culture of dominion, plays an integrated maintenance function in the established social order. The laws it constructs don't save animals' lives if the purpose of a given industry is to sell or use up those lives. The laws extend no kindnesses to animals where doing so would substantially cut into profit. They are designed to accept rather than challenge the use of animals. Professionalized animal-welfare advocacy will typically seize upon narrowly focused, short-term efforts, and will measure its successes in terms of media attention, increased membership, wealth, status, and the lobbying power of the organizations that achieve them. These factors work in conflict with the goals of animal-rights advocates. Because they concentrate on negotiating terms with lawmakers and businesses, rather than the underlying power of people themselves, their negotiated terms can be easily repealed or modified to suit industry preferences.

Animal-welfare modifications, by their very nature, don't encourage meaningful lifestyle change. Animal use industries are keenly aware of this. Industry supporters can articulate the difference between, on the one hand, extending measures of humane welfare within a system of use and, on the other hand, positing a challenge to the system of use itself. Industry knows these two ideas are distinct.

Advocates don't always know. Welfare societies not only work to forge what they call win-win situations with government and industry; they also work to convince animal-rights activists to join in the effort. To the extent that they succeed (a phenomenal extent, so far), they render the movement too timid – or, as they might prefer to say, pragmatic – to ask for what it wants. A casual glance at a few advocacy websites will demonstrate the vastness of the problem, inevitably with real effects for real animals.

The use of force causes strikingly parallel problems, arising from the same pragmatism and a similar interest in animals already domesticated, trained, or confined. Authoritarian activism often looks for the worst conditions of use. It becomes the welfare industry's shadow, the vigilante component to the culture of enforcement that the humane community directs. Marine mammal advocate Paul Watson explains that he founded the Malibu, California-based Sea Shepherd Conservation Society in 1977 not to protest, but to oppose poachers, "industrial over-fishing," and whale kills that violate international law. "We only damage property being used in illegal things," Watson has said. "We're actually more like a police organization than anything else."[1]

Radical activism would not mean accepting the function of opposing horrors, but rather going to the root of the problem, dissuading the public from supporting animal-based business. Property destruction is as unlikely to do that as videotapes showing violations of the Marine Mammal Protection Act or the Animal Welfare Act. Setting out to oppose what's illegal and what's spectacular is a deliberate decision not to make radical change.

Social justice movements everywhere find guidance in the idea that another world is possible, and that once an idea can be conceived, it can be achieved. Theories can indeed be put into practice overnight, for example, by simply declining to buy what animal vendors are selling. With each person who decides to do that, a movement takes a step in the direction of ending oppressive industries and replacing them with life-affirming ones.

It's important to get serious, to ask for what we really want, and to work for meaningful change. For there's real terror to address. Outside our homes and offices, there's a procession of calves up the turnpike, a hundred thousand faces floating past us at night. In broad daylight, ice floes are breaking apart in the warmth of industrial success. Scientists are building mice with human brain cells, and *Time* magazine has declared a cloned Afghan dog an invention of the year. There's work to do. Let's uncage ourselves.

NOTES TO INTRODUCTION ∾ PAGES 11–20

1 Gerri Peev, "BNP and Animal Rights Activists Face House Arrest," *The Scotsman* (27 Jan. 2005), citing Stephen McCabe, an adviser to British Home Secretary Charles Clarke, as specifying that the broadening of measures already applied in cases of international terror suspects would affect right-wing groups and animal advocates.

2 Beth Pearson, "Charging the Cranks Won't Touch Terror," *The [Glasgow] Herald* (26 Oct. 2005).

3 Toby Helm, "Extremism Map 'Shows Rural Hot Spots'," *[London] Telegraph* (21 Sep. 2005).

4 E-mail from Win Animal Rights ("CentCom at War-Online"), "Please Thank Joan Dunayer and Contact Other Conference Speakers" (14 Apr. 2005). By the following day, the WAR missive would be backed by a second entity, a New Jersey-based group called The Animal Spirit, which characterized Potok as "a strong opponent of animal rights" and urged speakers to "withdraw from the conference." Message from Shell Sullivan to GREY2K USA (15 Apr. 2005).

5 Southern Poverty Law Center, "From Push To Shove," *Intelligence Report* (Issue 107; Autumn 2002).

6 *See, e.g.,* Al Martinez, "Blood and Mayhem, All in the Name of Our Furry Friends," *Los Angeles Times* (10 Nov. 2003).

7 An essay by Steven Best, "Who's Afraid of Jerry Vlasak?," confirms Vlasak's agreement with that comment and additionally quotes Vlasak's statement on Australian television in October 2004: "Would I advocate taking five guilty vivisectors' lives to save hundreds of millions of innocent animal lives? Yes, I would."

8 Chris Maag, "America's # 1 Threat (and His Little Dog, Too): Kevin Kjonaas of Stop Huntingdon Animal Cruelty)," *Mother Jones* (Vol. 31, Issue 1; 1 Jan. 2006).

9 One of the FBI's most wanted fugitives was sought in connection with firebombings at the Chiron Corporation. Sabotage at Chiron in August 2003 and at the Shaklee Corporation in September 2003 has been ascribed to the Revolutionary Cells, a group dedicated to "animal liberation through armed struggle."

10 Hugh R. Morley, "Animal Rights or Wrongs?" *NorthJersey.com* (30 Oct. 2005), quoting the company's top U.S. executive, Chief Financial Officer Richard Michaelson.

11 As quoted in John Cook, "Thugs for Puppies," *Salon.com* (7 Feb. 2006).

12 Bob Graham and Nicola Woolcock, "Huntingdon Animal Activists Face Terrorism Charges in U.S.," *The [London] Times* (22 Jan. 2005).

13 Count 1, "Overt Acts: The Attack on C. Corp.," page 21 of the indictment document. This is part of a list of allegations brought under the Animal Enterprise

Protection Act, for which conviction carries up three years in prison when, as in the SHAC case, the property damage claim exceeds $10,000. The group was also charged with conspiracy to engage in interstate stalking and three counts of interstate stalking, a law triggered when a person is put in "reasonable fear" of death or serious bodily injury. Three of the SHAC defendants were convicted on those counts. Each of those charges carries up to five years in prison and a $250,000 fine.

14 Bob Graham and Nicola Woolcock, "Huntingdon Animal Activists Face Terrorism Charges in U.S.," *The [London] Times* (22 Jan. 2005); John Cook, "Thugs for Puppies," *Salon.com* (7 Feb. 2006).

15 In April 2006, Reuters reported that Huntingdon had subsequently stopped trading on the Pink Sheets as well.

16 John Cook, "Thugs for Puppies," *Salon.com* (7 Feb. 2006).

17 David Kocieniewski, "Six Animal Rights Advocates Are Convicted of Terrorism," *New York Times* (3 Mar 2006).

18 John Cook, "Thugs for Puppies," *Salon.com* (7 Feb. 2006).

19 Jon Burstein, "Home Searched After Office Raid," *[Florida] Sun-Sentinel* (15 Jan. 2005).

20 Terri Judd, Animal Rights Extremists Target Dead Man's Family," *Belfast Telegraph* (15 Nov. 2005).

21 Quoted by Owen Bowcott, "Animal Rights Activists Target Chain of Children's Nurseries Linked to Lab," *The Guardian* (29 Sep. 2005).

22 "Nursery Severs HLS Links After Chilling Threats From Extremists," *Cambridge Evening News* (30 Sep. 2005) (quoting a letter obtained by Britain's *Channel 4 News).*

23 In the wake of a series of bombings in July 2005 in London, Britain's Home Office announced it would bar visitors who "foment, justify or glorify terrorist violence in furtherance of particular beliefs; seek to provoke others to terrorist acts; [or] foment other serious criminal activity or seek to provoke others to serious criminal acts." The British government thereby excluded Steve Best, discussed in Chapter One, from participating in an event to celebrate a farm owner's decision to stop breeding guinea pigs for experimental use. Donald MacLeod, "Britain Uses Hate Law to Ban Animal Rights Campaigner," *The Guardian* (31 Aug. 2005). For more detailed discussion of that event, *see* Chapter Ten, "Draconian Activism."

NOTES TO CHAPTER ONE ☙ PAGES 23–29

1 The Center for Consumer Freedom defines itself as "a nonprofit coalition of restaurants, food companies, and consumers working together to promote personal responsibility and protect consumer choices."

2 "Professor Criticized for Animal Rights Work," *El Paso Times* (19 May 2005).

3 Whether one accepts the argument that such conflicts are rare or not, it's hardly original. The title of Best's essay, in fact, is a take-off from a book that spends the better part of about 250 pages making the argument that few bona fide conflicts exist: Gary Francione's *Introduction to Animal Rights: Your Child or the Dog?* (Temple; 2000).

4 Michael Albert, "Raise Your Voice But Keep Your Head Down," *ZNet* (9 Feb. 2005).

5 Michael J. Murphy and John I.B McCulloch, "Gulf War Reveals Environmental Terrorist Threat," *National Underwriter Property & Casualty-Risk & Benefits Management* (Issue 17; 29 Apr. 1991).

6 *See* Paul Watson, "In Defense of Tree-Spiking," *Earth First! Journal* (22 Sep. 1990) (reprinted on the website of Industrial Workers of the World).

7 "The 'Good' Pirate: Interview with Capt. Paul Watson" (edited from a piece which first appeared in the Spring 2003 issue of *Bite Back* magazine and reprinted on Paul Watson's Sea Shepherd Conservation Society website).

8 Captain Paul Watson, Sea Shepherd Conservation Society Editorial: "Shepherd and Sailors, Pirates and Prophets" (undated).

NOTES TO CHAPTER TWO ∾ PAGES 31–35

1 Tom Regan, *The Case for Animal Rights* (University of California Press; 1983) at 324.

2 *See* Elizabeth Kolbert, *Field Notes From a Catastrophe* (Bloomsbury USA; 2006).

3 Climatologists who met at the British government's conference in February 2005 heard that a rise of just 2.1 degrees Celsius (3.8 Fahrenheit), almost certain to happen this century, will deprive as many as three billion people of the water needed to meet their basic needs. For a discussion of the ways in which U.S. security would be impacted by such change, see Peter Schwartz & Doug Randall, "An Abrupt Climate Change Scenario and Its Implications for U.S. National Security" (dated Oct. 2003 and released Feb. 2004), available from the Global Business Network, 5900-X Hollis Street, Emeryville, California 94608.

4 Activity in the United States generates approximately 24 percent of the world's extra greenhouse gases. *See generally* U.S. Dept. of Energy, Energy Information Administration, "Emissions of Greenhouse Gases in the United States 2003," Report #: DOE/EIA-0573 (2003) (released Dec. 13, 2004). This rough figure does not account for complexities such as the gas emitted elsewhere in the course of manufacturing products for the U.S. market.

5 *See* "National Program Annual Report: ARS Global Change National Program (204)" (FY 2001) *posted by* the U.S. Department of Agriculture, Agricultural Research Service, Jamie L. Whitten Building, 1400 Independence Ave., S.W., Washington D.C., 20250.

6 "Global Meat Consumption Has Far-Ranging Environmental Impacts," *World Watch Magazine* (Jul.-Aug. 2004), citing U.S. Department of Commerce figures.

7 Garrett Hardin had employed the lifeboat in a Malthusian argument called "Lifeboat Ethics." Seeing the burgeoning human population as outstripping the food supply that could sustain it, Hardin likened the top third of financially wealthy countries to a lifeboat which the less affluent people would like to enter, or from which they'd at least like to receive a share of the wealth. Hardin applied a consequentialist analysis, claiming that the net result of helping people would be catastrophic. Published as Garrett Hardin, "Lifeboat Ethics: the Case Against Helping the Poor," *Psychology Today* (Sep. 1974). Malthusian theory is based on the work of British economist Thomas Robert Malthus (1766-1834), who argued that population tends to increase faster than food supply, with inevitably disastrous results, unless checked by moral restraints, armed conflict, famine, or disease.

Along with author Paul Ehrlich, Hardin influenced a U.S. policy, carried out through international aid agencies, of high-pressure birth control promotion, including sterilization. Prompted by women's health activists, a broader family-planning and socio-economic agenda to reduce birth rates and lessen migratory pressures emerged at a United Nations Population Conference held in Cairo in 1994. The Sierra Club, the largest U.S. environmental lobbying group, subsequently dropped its support for immigration restriction and instead aligned its policy with efforts to improve the status of women and local living standards.

In recent years, however, the Sierra Club has faced an internal struggle for control, focused, in part, on calls for immigration restriction. The segment of the Club calling for immigration curbs – the Club's recent director Paul Watson being the most vocal among them – hail from the 1970s-era school of thought. Their position is criticized for missing the irony that the country with the highest waste and consumption levels, and the most resistant to change, would cite planetary resource limits as a reason to augment border control. Other critics, including the Southern Poverty Law Center, have published work detailing the connection between immigration restrictionists in the environmental movement and the influence of agitators who have held leadership roles with nativist or white supremacist groups. For more information on these issues, see Steven Rosenfeld, "Population Bombshell," *TomPaine.com* (5 Feb. 2004); "Hostile Takeover," *Intelligence Report* (Southern Poverty Law Center; Issue 113, Spring 2004); and Lee Hall, "Aliens on Spaceship Earth: The Controversial Sierra Club Elections," *Bender's Immigration Bulletin* (1 Jul. 2005).

8 As described in more detail elsewhere in this book, particularly in Chapters Six and Eight, precisely the same phenomenon pervades *illegal* activism. For the moment, the reader might consider an example relevant to the free-range egg campaigns. A group based in Rochester, New York known as Compassionate Consumers has a goal of convincing the Wegmans grocery chain to "phase out the use of cruel battery cages at its company-run egg farm" based on the concerns of customers who have

"expressed shock and disgust at the inhumane conditions at Wegmans Egg Farm" and "expect Wegmans to improve these conditions and go cage-free." Although successfully pressing the grocery to "go cage-free" would mean nothing certain except that customers will be paying more for the products of the egg industry, one of the group's activists, Adam Durand, faces a six-month trepassing sentence after breaking into the egg producer's building and filming the conditions.

NOTES TO CHAPTER THREE ✍ PAGES 37–46

1 I am indebted to Dr. Richard A. Koenigsberg, author of *Hitler's Ideology: A Study in Psychoanalytic Sociology* (Library of Social Science; 1975) for elucidation of this point.

2 The characterization of war as filicide appears in Aranaldo Rascovsky's "Filicide and the Unconscious Motivation for War," S.C. Feinstein and P.L. Giovacchini (eds.), *Adolescent Psychiatry: Developmental and Clinical Studies Volume 3* (Basic Books; 1973). The thesis of the chapter is that war, which increases in frequency as humans develop culture, is a system for the continuous sacrificial slaughter of children.

3 The freelance video journalist explained, "I did not work there to try to close it down, but I was shocked by what was going on and hope I'd find it a changed place if I went back there now." Zoe Broughton, "Seeing Is Believing: Cruelty to Dogs at Huntingdon Life Sciences," *The Ecologist* (March, 2001).

4 George D. Rodger, "Interview with Donald Watson," *The Vegan* (Summer 2003).

5 Moreover, a release of animals from commercial control can increase the number of animals used. The campaign against an English farm which supplied guinea pigs to a testing firm, further described in Chapter Ten, began in 1999 with a break-in at the farm in which 600 guinea pigs were realeased but a further 1,500 were reportedly killed because the break-in was deemed an unacceptable change in conditions. See David Powles, "End of Nightmare After Years of Hell: The Farmer," *Burton Mail* (13 May 2006).

6 A look at recent campaigns led by Newkirk's People for the Ethical Treatment of Animals shows one asking the KFC Corporation to press chicken suppliers to invest in gas chambers for "controlled-atmosphere killing" instead of continuing to use electrical stunning; another that urges a fur farm to use electrical stunning on chinchillas instead of cervical dislocation (because "cervical dislocation may not be an appropriate killing method because of the size of the chinchillas"); and still another that urges the killing of homeless cats and dogs by lethal injections instead of gas. Oddly juxtaposed against these campaigns is the group's mission statement, describing its work as "dedicated to establishing and protecting the rights of all animals."

NOTES TO CHAPTER FOUR ✍ PAGES 47–57

1 Nearly half of the state legislators in the United States have memberships in

ALEC, a group which has influenced hundreds of laws. *See* Edwin Bender, "Private Prisons, Politics & Profits" from the Institute on Money in State Politics (Jul. 1, 2000). A large proportion of ALEC's budget has come from donations from private corrections corporations. ALEC's Criminal Justice Task Force has been co-chaired by Brad Wiggins, director of business development for the Corrections Corporation of America, and Brian Nairin of the National Association of Bail Insurance Companies. Richard Locker, "Foes Sharpen Focus on Lamar's Finances," *The Commercial Appeal* (Feb. 18, 1996).

2 Neil Strassman, "Measure Targets Eco-Terrorism," *Fort Worth Star-Telegram* (20 Feb. 2003).

3 Mark Townsend, "Exposed: Secrets of the Animal Organ Lab," *The Observer* (20 Apr. 2003). The project pointed out a litany of traditional animal welfare discrepancies; but more important, it concluded that experiments leading to cross-species transplants ought never to have been undertaken at all. That a major newspaper would sum up the work as a serious challenge to the value of vivisection itself speaks to the thoroughness of the campaign, named Diaries of Despair, which was carried out by Dan Lyons and the Uncaged project.

4 George J. Annas, *Informed Consent to Human Experimentation: The Subject's Dilemma* 15-16 (Ballinger Publishing; 1977).

5 Mark Townsend, "Exposed: Secrets of the Animal Organ Lab," *The Observer* (20 Apr. 2003).

6 "How to avoid reducing animal rights to the rights of some people to speak for animals against the rights of other people to speak for the same animals needs further thought," writes Catharine A. MacKinnon in the chapter "Of Mice and Men: A Feminist Fragment on Animal Rights" in *Animal Rights: Current Debates and New Directions* (Cass R. Sunstein and Martha C. Nussbaum, eds., Oxford University Press; 2004), at 270 (internal citation omitted).

7 As quoted in David Bank, "Is a Chimp A Person With a Legal Right To a Lawyer in Court?", *The Wall Street Journal* (25 Apr. 2002).

8 The idea of the right to be let alone appeared in a 1890 *Harvard Law Review* article, wherein Samuel Warren and Louis Brandeis called the tort of battery "recognition of the legal value of sensations." See Samuel Warren and Louis Brandeis, "The Right to Privacy," 4 *Harvard Law Review* 193 (1890), at note 1 and surrounding text (crediting Judge Cooley for the phrase "right to be let alone" in Thomas M. Cooley's *A Treatise on the Law of Torts or the Wrongs Which Arise Independent of Contracts* (Callaghan; 1888 ed.)). In the wake of lurid media accounts of the social activities of a prominent Boston family, Warren and Brandeis proposed a new tort: the invasion of privacy. Distinguishing it from injury to reputation on grounds that invasion of the "the private life, habits, acts, and relations of an individual" damaged a person's sense of dignity and embittered one's life, the writers declared that the concern at issue was not confined to property rights, but rather focused on

an individual's "inviolate personality."

9 *Olmstead v. United States*, 277 U.S. 438, 478 (1928) (Brandeis J. dissenting).

10 Statement of Skip Boruchin, Legacy Trading Company, quoting the SHAC website, in U.S. Senate Committee on Environment & Public Works Hearing: Eco-terrorism (26 Oct. 2005).

11 Nick Fielding, "Animal Activists Put Children on Hitlist," *The [London] Sunday Times* (12 Sep. 2004), describing a five-page, unpublished communication dated July 2004.

12 *See* Jenifer Johnston, "Of Mice and Men," *Sunday Herald - Scotland* (19 Sep. 2004).

13 "Animal Activist Joan Plans Another Protest," *Cambridge Evening News* (15 Apr. 2005).

NOTES TO CHAPTER FIVE ᴇᴏ PAGES 59–60

1 As quoted in Anita Manning, "Animals May Hold the Answer," *USA Today* (14 Aug. 1996).

NOTES TO CHAPTER SIX ᴇᴏ PAGES 63–75

1 Jenifer Johnston, "Of Mice and Men," *Sunday Herald - Scotland* (19 Sep. 2004), quoting British ALF press officer Robin Webb.

2 Kevin Jonas (variously written as Kevin Kjonaas), "Trail-Blazing a Corporate Attack," *No Compromise* (Issue 24; Summer 2004).

3 Michael Parfit, "Earth First!ers Wield a Mean Monkey Wrench," *Smithsonian* (Vol. 21; Issue 1; Apr. 1990).

4 This quote from Watson's biography, posted on the Sea Shepherd Web site, appears in Dean Schabner, "Pirate or Policeman: High Seas Activist Says He Fights To Uphold Law," *ABC News.com* (electronic; 1 Aug. 2002).

5 Michael Parfit, "Earth First!ers Wield a Mean Monkey Wrench," *Smithsonian* (Vol. 21; Issue 1; Apr. 1990).

6 Captain Paul Watson, Sea Shepherd Conservation Society Editorial: "Shepherd and Sailors, Pirates and Prophets" (undated).

7 As quoted in "From Push to Shove," Southern Poverty Law Center's *Intelligence Report* (Issue 107; 2002).

8 Kevin Jonas (variously written as Kevin Kjonaas), "Trail-blazing a Corporate Attack," *No Compromise* (Issue 24; Summer 2004).

9 *See* Jim Hughes, "Eco-Terrorists Top FBI's List: Attacks Intensify Since Fires 5 Years Ago at Vail," *Denver Post* (19 Oct. 2003) (quoting an environmental activist).

10 According to an article by Iowa State University economists John Lawrence and Daniel Otto, published under the title "Economic Importance of the United

States Cattle Industry" by the National Cattlemen's Beef Association, the estimated $38 billion of gross output from beef production activity supports an additional $115 billion in economic output for a total of $153 billion of direct and indirect economic activity throughout the U.S. economy.

11 Helen Branswell, "Penning Poultry Indoors Doesn't Eliminate Risk of Bird Flu Spread: Officials," *Canadian Press* (24 Aug. 2005).

12 U.S. Newswire, "Trader Joe's Gives Birds Something to Sing About: The Humane Society of the United States & Trader Joe's Reach Agreement Affecting Hundreds of Thousands of Animals" (8 Nov. 2005).

13 This wording appears on the Florida-based *Bite Back* site as a general mission statement, just before the guidelines. It is positioned as the first of four in the Animal Liberation Guidelines listed by the Animal Liberation Front website at www.animalliberationfront.com (a site with a posted founding date of 1991 – the year that the ALF Press Office was founded as an entity distinct from the supporters' groups) and its linked site, that of the North American Animal Liberation Press Office. It also appears in numerous ALF support groups' literature. The full list of Guidelines on the Animal Liberation Front website is:

> *To liberate animals from places of abuse, i.e., laboratories, factory farms, fur farms, etc., and place them in good homes where they may live out their natural lives, free from suffering; To inflict economic damage to those who profit from the misery and exploitation of animals; To reveal the horror and atrocities committed against animals behind locked doors, by performing non-violent direct actions and liberations; To hold those who are responsible and complicitous in the abuse, torture and death accountable for the terrorism they commit against innocent, sentient non-human animals.*

14 This emphasis has undergone gradual change. Historical versions of the guidelines say "To liberate animals from suffering or potential suffering and place them in good permanent homes or, where appropriate, release them into their natural environment." Appropriateness, of course, is a tricky matter when confined animals are released. Mink releases have attracted much public comment, particularly regarding the tragic consequences experienced by the confused minks and the animals in their paths. Releases of domesticated or captive-bred animals have been the topics of parody.

15 Jenifer Johnston, "Of Mice and Men," *Sunday Herald - Scotland* (19 Sep. 2004).

16 *U.S. News & World Report* (8 Apr. 2002), quoting People for the Ethical Treatment of Animals president Ingrid Newkirk.

17 Catharine A. MacKinnon's essay "Of Mice and Men: A Fragment on Animal Rights" appears in *Women's Lives; Men's Laws* (Belknap-Harvard; 2005) at pages 91-102 and also appears as a "Feminist Fragment" in *Animal Rights: Current Debates and New Directions* (Cass R. Sunstein and Martha C. Nussbaum, eds., Oxford University Press; 2004) at pages 263-276.

18 Ingrid Newkirk, "PETA Statement at News Conference Regarding Euthanasia" (17 Jun. 2005). Distributed by Colleen O'Brien, Manager of Communications, People for the Ethical Treatment of Animals, after two of the organization's employees were charged in North Carolina with felony cruelty to animals in connection with bags, dumped in a refuse bin, that contained numerous dead dogs and puppies. The organization officially defended the killings as "euthanasia" while disapproving the method of disposal.

Numerous commentators, including Lawrence Finsen and Susan Finsen, in their 1994 book *The Animal Rights Movement in America: From Compassion to Respect* (Twayne Publishers), suggest that the advent of the campaign group People for the Ethical Treatment of Animals, along with the Animal Liberation Front, heralded a modern, respect-based animal-rights movement. It is becoming increasingly obvious that this position is subject to brisk refutation – in other words, a sensible argument would hold that the attitudes propelling these groups subverted rather than advanced an earlier abolitionist paradigm – but a thorough historical analysis must be left for another day.

NOTES TO CHAPTER SEVEN ∞ PAGES 77–80

1 1998 U.S. Terrorism Report (quoting 28 C.F.R. 0.85). The definitions from the U.S. Department of State and the Central Intelligence Agency define terrorism in the context of international conflict, and require that the terrorist act be committed against a "noncombatant" target. *See* 22 U.S.C.S. § 2656f(d) (2003). Implied here is that terrorism is targeted at persons who have no relation, or at most an indirect relation, to the grievance of the perpetrator.

2 Capitol Hill Hearing Testimony before the House Resources Subcommittee, Forest and Forest Health: "Eco-Terrorism and Lawlessness in the National Forests" (12 Feb. 2002), statement of James F. Jarboe, Domestic Terrorism Section Chief, FBI Counterterrorism Division.

In October 2001, with the still populace reeling from televised images of aircraft devastating the World Trade Towers, Congress hastily agreed to the "USA Patriot Act," a law raising prison sentences, broadening the legal definition of terrorism, and drawing outrage from leading Constitutional law scholars such as David Cole of Georgetown University.

3 Brent L. Smith, "Terrorism in America: Pipe Bombs and Pipe Dreams" in *New Directions in Crime and Justice Studies* (Albany State University of New York Press; 1994), at 5.

4 *Elfbrandt v. Russell*, 384 U.S. 11, 19 (1966).

5 The SHAC 7, "Who are the SHAC 7?" Available, when last visited 18 Mar. 2005, at: http://www.shac7.com/shac.htm

NOTES TO CHAPTER EIGHT ∾ PAGES 87–103

1 All text excerpted here was originally published in Jane van Lawick-Goodall, *In the Shadow of Man* (Houghton Mifflin; 1971) at 236-37 (emphasis in the original).

2 Public commentary (not to mention the "victory" announcements of animal advocates themselves) routinely focuses on husbandry issues and leave vast institutions of animal use unchallenged. The words of one outside observer mirror the claims of the animal-welfare advocates themselves:

> *But the biggest victory so far for the animal-rights movement came last October, when the U.S. Department of Agriculture (USDA) agreed to settle a lawsuit filed by a group called the Alternatives Research and Development Foundation that was seeking to expand the scope of the Animal Welfare Act of 1966. Since its passage, this act had been interpreted as empowering the U.S. Department of Agriculture to oversee the treatment in laboratory experiments of large animals like dogs, cats, and primates. Left out of this regulatory regime were birds and, most importantly, mice and rats, which account for 95 percent of all animals used in scientific tests.*

Damon Linker, "Rights for Rodents," *Commentary* (No. 4, Vol. 111; 1 Apr. 2001).

3 MacKinnon writes:

> *The hierarchy of people over animals is not seen as imposed by humans because it is seen as due to animals' innate inferiority by nature. In the case of men over women, it is either said that there is no inequality there, because the sexes are different, or the inequality is conceded but said to be justified by the sex difference, that is, women's innate inferiority by nature.*

Catharine A. MacKinnon, "Of Mice and Men: A Feminist Fragment on Animal Rights" in *Animal Rights: Current Debates and New Directions* (Cass R. Sunstein and Martha C. Nussbaum, eds., Oxford University Press; 2004) at 264. MacKinnon further notes that "[i]n place of recognizing the realities of dominance of humans over animals and men over women is a sentimentalization of that dominance…"

4 The statement is attributed to Dr. King in Steven Best and Anthony J. Nocella II, eds., *Terrorists or Freedom Fighters?* (Lantern Books; 2004) – including in an excerpt of the book formerly reprinted on the website of Best's papers – and again in a version of a 2004 interview published on the website of Best's papers as "The Epiphanies of Dr. Steven Best: Interview With Claudette Vaughn of *Vegan Voice*" (2004). No original source is cited in these writings. Although the book *Terrorists or Freedom Fighters?* directs readers to another book, *Green Rage* by Christopher Manes (Back Bay Books; 1991), that book likewise fails to provide an original source for the statement in King's writings or speeches.

5 Dr. Martin Luther King Jr., "I've Been to the Mountaintop," speech at Mason Temple (Memphis, Tenn.; 3 Apr. 1968), in support of sanitation workers who had been on strike since February. It was the final speech delivered by Dr. King, who was assassinated the next day.

6 Statement of Jerry Vlasak, in U.S. Senate Committee on Environment & Public Works Hearing: Eco-terrorism (26 Oct. 2005).

7 "Vlasak Dropped From Sea Shepherd Board," *Canadian Broadcasting Co.* (22 Apr. 2005).

8 "Violence Against Sealers OK: Activist," *Canadian Broadcasting Co.* (19 Apr. 2005).

9 The codification of their property status in the laws of the United States receives detailed treatment in Gary L. Francione, *Animals, Property, and the Law* (Temple; 1997).

10 In May 2006, intimidating letters were sent to small shareholders in drugs group GlaxoSmithKline, telling them to sell their shares or face having their details posted on the Internet. MSN, the Hotmail service operator, has said that the people who have sent the menacing e-mails to Glaxo shareholders may have their e-mail accounts suspended. *See* Melanie Reid, "Fighting Back Against Animal-Rights Bullies," *The [Glasgow] Herald* (Web Issue 2526; 11 May 2006).

11 FBI testimony to Congress in February 2002 on the Animal Liberation Front and Earth Liberation Front; "The Terrorist Threat Confronting the United States," Congressional Statement, Federal Bureau of Investigation. The accumulated economic damage attributed to animal and environmental advocacy is estimated at more than $100 million. Jim Hughes, "Eco-Terrorists Top FBI's List: Attacks Intensify Since Fires 5 Years Ago at Vail," *Denver Post* (19 Oct. 2003). But often, corporations will not publicize reports of damage or losses; Earth First! has estimated that sabotage has cost the timber industry as much as $25 million dollars in a single year. *See* Michael J. Murphy and John I.B McCulloch, "Gulf War Reveals Environmental Terrorist Threat," *National Underwriter Property & Casualty-Risk & Benefits Management* (Issue 17; 29 Apr. 1991).

12 Arnold authored the 1997 book *Ecoterror: The Violent Agenda to Save Nature* (Free Enterprise Press). Although closely associated with Arnold, the term Wise Use was first used by Gifford Pinchot, who headed the U.S. Forest Service under Theodore Roosevelt. Arnold employs the term to aggressively lobby for the transfer of public land to private interests. In the 2005 book *Divine Destruction : Dominion Theology and American Environmental Policy* (Melville House), Stephenie Hendricks discusses an interview with Robert Kennedy, Jr. on Arnold's matchmaking between the Christian right and the industries that stand to lose money because of environmental protections.

13 Katherine Long, "His Goal: Destroy Environmentalism; Man and Group Prefer That People Exploit the Earth," *Seattle Times* (2 Dec. 1991), quotes Arnold as saying, "Our goal is to destroy, to eradicate the environmental movement . . . We're mad as hell. We're not going to take it anymore. We're dead serious – we're going to destroy them." Ellipse in original. This quote is not unusual, but representative of a number of statements in Arnold's media interviews.

14 *See* Steven Best, "It's War! The Escalating Battle Between Activists and the Corporate-State Complex" (2004) (internal citations omitted).

15 Judith Lewis, "Earth to ELF: Come In, Please," *Los Angeles Weekly* (23-29 Dec. 2005).

16 Tom Regan, "ACLU Accuses FBI of 'Spying' on Activists," *Christian Science Monitor* (19 May 2005).

17 Jack Lessenberry, "Activist Devotes Life to Animal Rights," *The Toledo Blade* (24 Jun. 2001).

18 See Yi-Fu Tuan, *Domination and Affection: The Making of Pets* (Yale; 1984). We have produced most breeds of cats and dogs in the era of late capitalism, and modern dogs owe their distinctive appearances to intensive breeding in just the last 500 years. See Leslie A. Lyons, PhD, "Developing Genetic Management Programs for Feline Breeds," Proceedings of the Tufts' *Canine and Feline Breeding and Genetics Conference* (2003); Peter Savolainen et al., "Genetic Evidence for an East Asian Origin of Domestic Dogs," *Science* 1610-1613 (Vol. 298; Nov. 22, 2002) (also suggesting that the myriad breeds of pet dogs originated in just a handful of wolves tamed by humans living in or near China less than 15,000 years ago).

19 Iowa State University's updated estimates for 2004, as recorded in the International Lamb Industry Profile.

20 "Tests: Activists Fed Pork to Sheep," *CNN*, from the Associated Press (4 Dec. 2003). Some activists who supported Hahnheuser cited Section 5 of Australia's Terrorism Insurance Act of 2003, which exempts certain conduct from the definition of economic terrorism if it is not intended to create a serious health or safety risk, and claiming that Hahnheuser had in fact created no safety risk. There is a stark irony here, given vegetarians' own concerns over possibilities of food contamination. The relevant decision-makers apparently did see a safety risk. The 1,800 sheep who "came into contact" with the shredded pig flesh were slaughtered for pet food.

21 This point is discussed in Steve Baker's essay "Picturing the Beast: Animals, Identity and Representation" (Manchester University Press; 1993).

22 Michael Parfit, "Earth First!ers Wield a Mean Monkey Wrench," *Smithsonian* (Vol. 21; Issue 1; Apr. 1990).

NOTES TO CHAPTER NINE ∽ PAGES 105–114

1 The quotes in this section derive from Steven Best, "It's War! The Escalating Battle Between Activists and the Corporate-State Complex" (2004).

2 Excerpted from "HSUS in Action, Trotting Along: Help for Horses," *All Animals*, published by the Humane Society of the United States (Fall 2005), at page 12.

3 Humane Society of the United States press release: "Plan To Increase Wild Horse

Contraception Announced" (30 Nov. 2005).

4 The natural ancestor of modern cattle, the aurochs, went extinct in 1627, when the one thought to be the last surviving member of the species was killed by a poacher in Poland.

5 The husband was defined as the master of the household, and, as her legal guardian, could subject his wife to corporal punishment if she defied his authority. Blackstone's treatise on the English common law stated:

For, as he is to answer for her misbehavior, the law thought it reasonable to intrust him with this power of restraining her, by domestic chastisement, in the same moderation that a man is allowed to correct his apprentices or children; for whom the master or parent is also liable in some cases to answer. But this power of correction was confined within reasonable bounds....

The notion of the rule of thumb in the domestic violence context implicates a case called *State v. Rhodes* (1867), in which a spouse was let off because "His Honor was of opinion that the defendant had a right to whip his wife with a switch no larger than his thumb." Prosser's first handbook stated, referring to the same case, "It was said that not even the criminal law would interfere, if he beat her with a stick no thicker than his thumb." The 1897 edition of Blackstone said that "the Supreme Court, of North Carolina, declared in *State v. Rhodes* . . . that a husband has a right to whip his wife with 'a stick as large as his finger but not larger than his thumb.' This decision was in recognition of a barbarous custom which modern authorities condemn." In fact, the court's declaration in Rhodes was repudiated by the state supreme court in 1868.

In *Bradley v. State*, an 1824 Mississippi case, Powhattan Ellis, for the supreme court, commented on corporal punishment:

[A]n unlimited licence of this kind cannot be sanctioned, either upon principles of law or humanity. It is true, according to the old law, the husband might give his wife moderate correction, because he is answerable for her misbehaviour; hence it was thought reasonable, to intr[u]st him, with a power, necessary to restrain the indiscretions of one, for whose conduct he was to be made responsible. . . . Sir William Blackstone says, during the reign of Charles the first, this power was much doubted.–Notwithstanding the lower orders of people still claimed and exercised it as an inherent privilege, which could not be abandoned, without entrenching upon their rightful authority, known and acknowledged from the earliest periods of the common law, down to the present day. I believe it was in a case before Mr. Justice Raymond, when the same doctrine was recognised, with proper limitations and restrictions, well suited to the condition and feelings of those, who might think proper to use a whip or rattan, no bigger than my thumb, in order to inforce the salutary restraints of domestic discipline. I think his lordship might have narrowed down the rule in such a manner, as to restrain the exercise of the right, within the compass of great moderation, without producing a destruction of the principle itself. If the defendant now before us, could shew from the record in this case, he confined himself

within reasonable bounds, when he thought proper to chastise his wife, we would deliberate long before an affirmance of the judgment.

Quoted in Henry Ansgar Kelly, "Rule of Thumb and the Folklaw of the Husband's Stick," *Journal of Legal Education*, Vol. 44, at 341 (1994).

6 In *Fulgham v. State* (1871), Judge Peters of North Carolina referred to this customary measurement, albeit not approvingly.

7 A book published by Humane Society of the United States provides the following commentary, in question-and-answer format:

Is it right to manipulate a wild animal's reproductive system, and potentially its behavior, for human purposes? ...The public demands that action be taken when public health, safety, or subsistence are threatened by wildlife. Not only is this view ethically defensible, but (more to the point) it is also widespread, and we do not see this consensus changing in our lifetimes.

Quoting Kirkpactrick and Ruthberg, "Fertility Control in Animals," in *The State of the Animals* 2001 (Humane Society Press; 2001).

8 Open letter from Fred O'Regan, President, International Fund for Animal Welfare, entitled "IFAW Demands Apology from Canadian Politician" (8 Mar. 2006); *see also* Rob Antle, "Williams Rejects TV Debate With IFAW President," *The [St. John's] Telegram* (17 Mar. 2006).

9 It's likely that the U.S. Humane Society will publicly disapprove of the threats of violence; my claim here is not that mainstream animal-welfare groups act like militants, but the reverse: that is, that militant groups espouse mainstream ideas rather than demonstrate a different paradigm. The fish boycott campaign promoted by Watson's Sea Shepherd Conservation Society treats marine animals simply as one consumer market to be pitted against another, belying the claim, recounted in Chapter One of this book, that Watson seeks to elucidate the "biocentric" perspective. As for those claiming to communicate for the ALF, the more they welcome violent tactics, the more conservative their campaigns seem to be, as seen in the alignment of their goals in this case with that of the world's wealthiest humane advocacy group.

10 Brian T. Murray, "Experiment at Jackson Safari Park Is Part of State Effort to Find an Alternative to Hunting," *Star-Ledger* (8 Oct. 2004).

11 David Ehrenfeld, *The Arrogance of Humanism* (Oxford University Press; 1981; after the earlier publication dated 1978) at 263.

12 Dale D. Goble and Eric T. Freyfogle, *Wildlife Law* (2002), preface page v. Although courts have applied stringent tests for standing in cases on behalf of non-human animals – most notably in *Lujan v. Defenders of Wildlife* 504 U.S. 555 (1992) – successful arguments have been presented that cognizable environmental impact can be incurred by animals themselves. In *Progressive Animal Welfare*

Society v. Department of the Navy, where plaintiffs maintained that 100 Atlantic bottle-nosed dolphins captured and moved by the Navy would be isolated in single holding pens and exposed to extremely cold water, the U.S. District Court for the Western District of Washington held that the National Environmental Policy Act of 1969 (NEPA) required the Navy to prepare a "reverse" environmental impact statement before dispatching dolphins at a nuclear submarine base. 725 F. Supp. 475, 476-79 (W.D. Wash. 1989). In the court's view, dolphins are an integral part of the environment and a decision to use them was a major federal action under the NEPA that required an analysis of effects on the dolphins themselves.

13 Environmental law to date would not necessarily contradict this goal. While the National Environmental Policy Act (NEPA) acknowledges the value of aesthetics to the quality of human life (*see* 42 U.S.C. § 4331(b) (1994) (declaring national goal to, among other things, "assure for all Americans safe, healthful, productive, and esthetically and culturally pleasing surroundings")), it also envisions humanity as living in harmony with our environment. *See* § 4321 (purposes of NEPA include "encourag[ing] productive and enjoyable harmony between man and his environment").

NOTES TO CHAPTER TEN ᴄ⌐ PAGES 115–128

1 Hugh R. Morley, "Animal Rights or Wrongs?", *NorthJersey.com* (30 Oct. 2005).

2 *Teva Pharmaceuticals v. Stop Huntingdon Animal Cruelty*, Docket No. C-63-05, Superior Court of New Jersey (3 Feb. 2006), denying SHAC's motion for reconsideration of a prior ruling denying its request for a jury trial.

3 This quote comes from "News From the Frontlines," *Bite Back* (14 Mar. 2005), with misspellings in the source.

4 The details described here were reported in "Family Under Siege," *BBC News* (18 Oct. 2004); Bob Graham and Nicola Woolcock, "Huntingdon Animal Activists Face Terrorism Charges in U.S.," *The [London] Times* (22 Jan. 2005); Nick Britten, "Animal Rights Protesters Face 12 Years Over Grave Robbery Plot," *[London] Telegraph* (11 Apr. 2006); Nicola Woolcock, "Animal Activists Face Jail Over Plot to Steal Body," *The [London] Times* (11 Apr. 2006); and Nick Britten, "Fourth Animal Activist Admits Fear Campaign," *[London] Telegraph* (12 Apr. 2006).

5 Staffordshire Police set up a unit of 20 detectives and spent more than £2.5 million protecting the farm from protesters, hundreds of thousands of pounds on the grave desecration investigation. See Nicola Woolcock, "Animal Activists Face Jail Over Plot to Steal Body," *The [London] Times* (11 Apr. 2006).

6 The details are discussed in "Twelve Years Each for Animal Rights Extremists," *Ireland Online*, an electronic outlet of British Telecom (11 May 2006); and David Powles, "Forty Years Jail for Animal Activists, *Burton Mail* (12 May 2006). According to a report on 11 May 2006 in London's *Daily Mail*, the toy was Hammond's grandchild's.

7 Quoted in Nicola Woolcock, "Animal Activists Face Jail Over Plot to Steal Body," *The [London] Times* (11 Apr. 2006).

8 Additional public sources consulted regarding the search for Gladys Hammond's body and the "victory parade" appear in Jonathan Brown, "Desecration of Grave Claimed as Victory for Animal Rights," *The Independent Online* (12 Oct. 2004); "Search Resumes in Body Theft Case," BBC News (18 May 2005); and "Five Arrests in 'Victory' Parade," *Burton Mail* (5 Sep. 2005).

9 Sandro Contenta, "Police Believe Corpse Was the Target of a Radical Campaign for Animal Rights in Britain," *Toronto Star* (9 Oct. 2005).

10 In this, the first ever successful use of conspiracy-to-blackmail charges against animal advocates, the judge could avoid considering a series of charges and instead contemplate a single, serious charge for each defedant which encompassed the entire campaign, and sentence each to a period of up to fourteen years. The Director of Public Prosecutions, Ken Macdonald QC, said, "This case sets a marker. CPS Prosecutors are using the law to its fullest extent to ensure that animal rights extremists involved in serious crime are eligible for very long sentences of imprisonment." Crown Prosecution Service Press Release: "CPS Charging Strategy in Darley Oaks Case Leads To Long Sentences" (11 May 2006). Nick Britten's series of reports in London's *Telegraph* (12 Apr. 2006) discusses the circumstances surrounding the guilty pleas of Josephine Mayo, Kerry Whitburn, Jon Ablewhite, and John Smith. Through liaison with the U.S. Embassy in London and the FBI, Staffordshire detectives used U.S. anti-terrorism legislation able to secure evidence from Ablewhite's library Hotmail account from Microsoft. "Twelve Years Each for Animal Rights Extremists," *Ireland Online*, an electronic outlet of British Telecom (11 May 2006). Although the prosecution did not prove the four actually removed the remains, the four did admit to using the act as part of a blackmail campaign. Two of the activists had also been charged in connection with aggressive actions against Huntingdon's managing director Brian Cass or Cass's family. Ablewhite, Smith and Whitburn were jailed for twelve years each and Mayo for four.

11 *See* Sentencing Guidelines Council, Guideline Judgments Case Compendium (London; Mar. 2005) (discussing a contested case addressing manslaughter by reason of provocation under the Homicide Act of 1957). In the same document, the Council writes, "In choosing a fair and just sentence in a particular case, judges and magistrates, within the parameters established by Parliament, must have regard to the gravity of the offence, its impact on the victim, the circumstances of the offender and the wider public interest."

12 Carl Dinnen, "RIP at Last?" *Channel 4 News London* (3 May 2006).

13 Nicola Woolcock, "Animal Rights Activists Surrender Stolen Body," *The [London] Times* (4 May 2006).

14 Nick Britten, "Animal Rights Gang Jailed for Twelve Years to Deter 'Lunatics',"

[London] Telegraph (12 May 2006). Smith did not admit to actually disinterring the remains.

15 "Masked Attackers Beat Huntingdon Boss," *The Guardian* (23 Feb. 2001). A person who came to the aid of Cass and gave chase was sprayed with tear gas. "Jail for Lab Boss Attacker," *BBC News* (16 Aug. 2001).

16 Information on this incident appears in "Phytopharm Loses Canaccord as Broker After Attack," *Bloomberg News Service* (23 Jun. 2005); and Sandra Laville and Duncan Campbell, "Animal Rights Extremists in Arson Spree," *The Guardian* (25 Jun. 2005).

17 Nicholas Pyke, "Campaigners Force Auditors to Quit Animal Testing Firm," *The Guardian* (1 Mar. 2003).

18 *See* Tony Blair, "Time to Act Against Animal Rights Protesters," *[London] Sunday Telegraph* (14 May 2006).

19 Jenifer Johnston, "Of Mice and Men," *Sunday Herald - Scotland* (19 Sep. 2004).

20 Although poll results on the subject vary, a widely reported 2005 Mori poll suggests that most people accept the use of nonhuman animals in medical research if they believe there is no unnecessary suffering. Professionalized welfare advocacy does not challenge that view, but instead reinforces it, attempting to win public support by investigating suspected cases of egregious abuse. Militants often follow this pattern, holding up legal welfare violations as justifications for their actions. Yet the rise in militant tactics – specifically those involving death threats, vandalism, targeting personnel and advertising their personal details on the Internet, and shouting abuse at people thought to be involved in animal use – has resulted in a major setback in the public's view of animaladvocacy, according to a survey carried out by YouGov for London's daily *Telegraph* in May 2006. An overwhelming 77 percent said it was right to call people such as those who carried out the campaign against the Darley Oaks farm "terrorists," against 15 percent who said it was not (while 8 percent did not know).

21 *See, for example*, Mary O'Hara, "Animal Rights Bomb Sent to Charity Shop," *The Guardian* (1 Feb. 2001) (describing such letters being read in court in reference to an animal-welfare campaign). Numerous articles refer to the use of the word "scum" by animal-welfare militants.

22 Michael Holden and Matthew Jones, "Britain Still Centre of Animal Rights 'Terrorism,'" Reuters (published in *The Scotsman* on 11 May 2006).

23 Discussion of the proposal in the autumn of 2005 appears in Beth Pearson, "Charging the Cranks Won't Touch Terror," *The [Glasgow] Herald* (Web Issue 2384; 26 Oct. 2005).

24 In Nazi Germany, any action was justifiable if it served to eliminate the forces working to destroy the body politic. Hitler's ideology, according to psychologist

Richard Koenigsberg, revolved around the fantasy of Germany as a living organism containing virulent Jewish micro-organisms. Genocide was undertaken as a form of immunology: a struggle to kill off pathogenic cells in order to save the organism. *See* Richard A. Koenigsberg, "Why Do Ideologies Exist? The Psychological Function of Culture" (electronic publication; 2005).

25 Adam Nicolson, "Animal Rights and Wrongs: The Campaign Against the Newchurch Guinea Pig Farm May Have Shocked, but Nelson Mandela Would Understand It," *The Guardian* (24 Aug. 2005).

26 For example, over a two-year period, Staffordshire police responded to more than 450 incidents relating to the Darley Oaks farm in Newchurch. Nicola Woolcock, "Animal Rights Activists Surrender Stolen Body," *The [London] Times* (4 May 2006).

27 "Staying Free and Avoiding the Activist Hall of Shame," *No Compromise*, "the militant, direct action publication of grassroots animal liberationists and their supporters" (Issue 25, Fall 2004).

28 George D. Rodger's December 2002 interview with Donald Watson, founder of the Vegan Society, was first published in *The Vegan* (Summer 2003).

NOTES TO CHAPTER ELEVEN ∾ PAGES 129–132

1 Lauran Neergaard (Associated Press), "Bonobos Settle Problems by Having Sex," *Fort Worth Star-Telegram* (11 May 1998).

2 *See* "Bonobos Settle Problems by Having Sex," ibid. Frans de Waal's 1997 book *Bonobo: The Forgotten Ape* (University of California Press) was one of the first to focus on bonobos.

3 Danny Postel's "Interview with Noel Ignatiev" was originally broadcast on WZRD-FM Radio in Chicago (17 Mar. 1996).

4 Elizabeth Fisher, *Woman's Creation: Sexual Evolution and the Shaping of Society* (Anchor/Doubleday; 1979).

5 *See* "Men and Women, Hunters and Gatherers," in Kevin Reilly, *The West and the World: A History of Civilization* (Harper and Row; 1989).

6 Examples mentioned in this section are discussed by Seeds for Change in its training and support to grassroots campaigners, co-ops and groups in the social sector.

NOTES TO EPILOGUE ∾ PAGES 135–138

1 Dean Schabner, "Pirate or Policeman: High Seas Activist Says He Fights To Uphold Law," *ABC News.com* (electronic; 1 Aug. 2002).

Index